This book gives detailed account of each Herb, its medicinal and curative properties, Western Herbalism, Chinese Herbalism, Herbalism and Homeopathy.

It throws ample light on the herbal treatment of various common disorders such as Asthma, Gout, Arthritis, Rheumatism, Migraine, Insomnia and various nervous disorders etc.

It also enlightens us about preventive & curative treatment for various common infants & children diseases.

The book has been written with the purpose that the common man should be in a position to cure himself, his family members and others also, at bare minimum expense and, above all, without any side-effects.

HERBAL CURE
FOR
COMMON DISEASES

Acharya Vipul Rao

DIAMOND BOOKS

ISBN : 81-7182-101-4

© Publisher

Publisher	: **Diamond Pocket Books (P) Ltd.**
	X-30, Okhla Industrial Area, Phase-II
	New Delhi-110020
Phone	: 011-51611861
Fax	: 011-51611866
E-mail	: sales@diamondpublication.com
Website	: www.diamondpublication.com
Edition	: 2005
Price	: Rs. 95/-
Printed at	: Adarsh Printers,
	Navin Shahdara, Delhi-110032

Herbal Cure For Common Diseases   **Rs. 95/-**
by Acharya Vipul Rao

Introduction

Use of herbs as a Vehicle for treating and even curing various diseases, which afflicted human race, is not a novel concept nor has it been discovered recently – its journey from Darwinian age to recent time is a long story of gradual progression and development. When modern sophisticated medicine had not emerged even or made its presence felt, every household treated the house mates with home remedies– the bulk of which was formed by herbs. It is a simple principle of diet that vegetations that grow on a particular soil, in a particular area, are capable of meeting dietary and medicinal needs of the local inhabitants. That is why so much emphasis was laid, and still is being laid on 'regional diet'. If you change over to regional diet, there is no reason, why should you fall ill.

The wisdom of cure, through medicinal herbs, has its history of turbulance, progress, regression and even resistance from certain sects who refrained from using certain herbs due to their bad, appearance, bad taste, foul smell, element of pungence, astringency, etc. It is a journey which has undergone many pitfalls. Efforts were made to scuttle and throttle progress of this unique system of curability but, despite all such bottlenecks and impediments, herbs always found a prestigious place in our homes. Repugnance of garlic and onion is simply due to their bad smell – to quote simply one instance; but medicines prepared out of these ingredients, freely used. It is sheer Hypocrisy and nothing else. Beet is not used as its hue resembles colour of blood, ginger is not used in some homes due to its pungent and disagreeable taste.

Now the pendulum has swayed the other way round. The change-over to herbal treatment is quite natural as it is more patient friendly and, to a greater extent, cost-effective also, and reaction is also minimal, to say the least. Moreover, the knowledge of herbs descended to new generations in the form of herbal heritage. There are still some families which cure even the so-called incurable disorders or really incurable disorders by using simply some herbs or even a single herb. They have formulations of their own which, for inexplicable reasons, are not being divulged to the common man – perhaps fear psychosis of generalisation or/and commercialisation might have prompted such persons to withhold their inherited knowledge.

Herbal treatment, herbal beauty care, herbal hair-dye, herbal massage, herbal oils, herbal tea etc are some of the oft-heard terms which is a clear and welcome sign pointing out to acceptance, adherance and usage of herbs in one form or the other. You can see herbalists spread over length and breath of this vast universe. European countries have now started researching on some herbs which, in their view, could stand as substitutes for the modern medicine which has its own merits and demerits.

This book has been written, keeping in view limitations of modern systems of medicine, not to speak of health hazards, side-effects, reactions, drug interactions emanating from use of drugs, so that the common man is in a position to cure himself, his family members and others also, at bare minimum expense and, above all, without any (or minimal) side-effects. It is a generally accepted view that Ayurvedic medicines have no side-effects nor are they harmful, though this is qualified eulogisation of this system's efficacy. any drug/herb used indiscreetly, imprudently and beyond a particular limit is liable to react on the user.

I have tried to give detailed account of each herb, its combining effect with other herbs, its side-effects and reactions, where possible, and have taken care to see that readers actually benefit from the details provided so that they could cure their kith and kin, well in time and also without straining pockets. No doubt, certain herbs are costly for an average buyer but there are less costlier substitutes therefor also. Most of the herbs are not new to our household, as those are used frequently to dispel common disorders but some herbs may be new to them, as herbal field is too vast – each region, country abounding only in particular varieties.

Diseases have been mentioned in relation to each herb, as each herb has multiple applications and uses. It is suggested that entire book is read in 1-2 sittings and specific points and portions of interest may be marked so that, in case of emergency, quick reference could be made to the relevant portion only. For convenience of the readers, Hindi names of Herbs have been explained, where possible and a list at the end of the book will spell out as to which herb is suitable for which disease(s). Shri Narender Kumar, Managing Director of Diamond Pocket Books, has been kind enough, as usual, to assist me by giving his matured advice and suggestions, despite his awful busy schedule.

— **Acharya Vipul Rao**

Caution

**U**se of herbal preparations, in any form, is considered to be a safe way to healthy life, but herbs and herbal preperations can cause reactions to certain individuals under specific conditions. Hence indiscreet use of any herbal medicine is fraught with dangerous consequences, as is the case with other systems of healing. We wish to warn our readers to consult a qualified and experienced herbalist for proper guidance in respect of diseases which they suffer from. Moreover, it would be wrong to conclude that all the diseases on earth can be controlled by herbal treatment, as this system has also its own limitations. The author and the publisher shall in no way be responsible if someone suffers inspite of this tacit warning.

— **Publisher**

CONTENTS

(1)
Herbs And Modern Medicine

In old days herbs were collected from the jungles, hills, plains, riverside beds and strenuous effort was required to collect even the bare minimum numbers of herbs which a person normally required to cure certain ailments. His collection was need-based. Means of communication were sparse which fact obliged a person to confine his needs and knowledge to the availability of herbs in his own area or in the areas in the vicinity of his surroundings.

Modern medicine lays stress on effect of a disorder, rather than seek or even attempt to know the cause. A medical herbalist will treat the patient holistically, treating the cause first and, when cause has been eradicated, disease will automatically get cured. Ayurveda System is the prominent user of herbs and its basic theory revolves round imbalance and Vitiation of three humors (Doshas). According to it when the three humors are fully balanced, a person will not take to illness but, when the humors get vitiated and disturbed, diseased condition surfaces. Further, Ayurvedic theory lays stress on the fact that plants and herbs (say vegetations) growing on a specific soil of a particular region are capable of curing ailments of the residents of the subject area. Theory of cause and effect forms basis of diagnosis in Ayurvedic and Homeopathic systems. Cause is a forerunner of effect. Modern medicine strikes at the root of effect, without laying much or no emphasis on cause. In Allopathy infection, allergy and climatic changes, dietary patterns, virus or bacteria are considered to be the factors (causes/situations) that trigger a disease. A Homeopath will focus his attention on causes, aggravations and ameliorations, desires and aversions, mental state while taking up a case. He will try to build up resistance capacity of the patient so that his body is made so strong as to fight with the monster of disease.

To claim that herbs could treat all the ailments which inflict humanity will be simply a misplaced notion, myth which defy truth. No system of medicine can claim like that, and herbal treatment is no exception to this tenet. Popularity and efficacy of a system is determined by the actual success rate, as achievement and success cannot be substituted by tall claims. To say that herbs are infallible, can cure any disease on earth, have no reaction and side-effects, are easy to obtain or are cost-effective are another tall and boasted claims. Any medicine that is capable of curing a disorder can equally be reactive, harmful, when used without cause, need, beyond specific duration, in excess of recommended dose and let there be no doubt about this stark reality.

"Herb is a plant whose stem is not woody or persistent. (It is) a plant, of which leaves etc are used for food, medicine, scent, flavour etc." If we take cognizance of this definition then all plantations/vegetations cannot be described and clubbed under herbs. Further, all herbs are not meant to serve medicinal purposes. There are certain herbs which are useful, while others are not meant for human use. A herb which is useful for one person, whether in health or disease, cannot be guaranteed to equally benefit the other person, the reason being that Prakriti (Nature) of each person is different and each herb acts/reacts according to status of one's Prakriti and resistance power. Herbs have high rate of curability, healing power and less side-effects. Herbs help to maintain a high role in balancing various processes in the body, promote general well-being and health. They are both corrective, curative and preventive, natural Vehicles and can be relied upon fully due to their minimal side-effects and reactions, of course barring a few which are to be used cautiously, sparingly, or never at all.

Herbs are part and parcel of our homes but, despite this much research is still required to be carried out as the work done, so far, fails to match the research work done in other medicinal systems. Modern medicine cannot be oblivous to the curing capability of herbs and that's the reason more and more research on herbs like Ashwagandha, Triphala, Neem, Banyan, Garlic, Turmeric, Holy Basil (Tulsi) Kankari, Parsley, saffron, Alfalfa, Jamun, Peepal, Onion, Fenugreek, Clove, Cariander, Cardamom, Cumin seeds, aniseed, vasaka, Henna, Saffron, Castor seeds, turmeric, linseed, Rhubarb, Arjun, ginseng, Pepper etc–to name a few only–still form part of many Indian homes. I have deliberately mentioned most names in Hindi.

Garam Masala, used in our Kitchens, is an excellent blend of spices and herbs which need no introduction as to their utility and efficacy. Their abundant and frequent use in our daily diet, various delicacies, other preparations bears testimony to the fact that neither herbs are new to us nor are we recent users of herbs.

Not only on human beings but also on animals, herbal treatment has been in vogue since time immemorial. Applying mustard oil and turmeric powder on wounds of horses and other pet animals is still an accepted practice. The animals are berefit of intelligent reasoning but are blessed with intuition which provides them a discriminatory sense, fortified by their smelling power to distinguish between what is worth accepting or rejecting. No one can force an animal to eat against its wish, though he is not blessed with reasoning and discriminative faculty but man, even though prosessing the aforesaid traits, falls ill due to indicreet act of overeating. The animals cure their diseases by plants, herbs and water, though they were never taught about healthy living and health care.

VEGETABLE KINGDOM

Plant is a part and parcel of vegetable Kingdom which includes trees, shrubs, bushes, vegetables, flowers, fruits, dry fruits, herbs etc. It is the small and tiny plant that ultimately grows into a big tree but certain plants do not have high growth rate. In fact, all the vegetations grow out of plants. There are creepers also which grow with the help of other big plants or trees. Plant kingdom is so vast and varied that, even now, most of the herbs are still unknown to us. What we know uptil now is merely a fraction of the total vegetable kingdom. Plants that grow under the river beds/oceans is still an enigma. It is said plants growing underneath water exceed far more than the plants that grow on earth or it could be the other way round also but existence of unknown varieties growing under the bottom of water cannot be denied.

Wise old phrases like 'less is more' and 'everything in moderation', apply equally to herbal medicine also. If you use only a part of a plant, where whole plant is to be used, you are not likely to derive any/desired benefit, as you have violated the basic tenet pertaining to use of that plant. The more plant material you use, the quicker and better benefits you would reap, because in this way natural balance of the plant is maintained. It is no use nor is it wise to use more pills of a herbal preparation (when part of plant has been used). This way you will simply upset the balance of your body and cause more harm to your body.

Plant world is so wide, vast and varied that you must consult some good and qualified herbalist, doctor or plant expert to know effects of a particular plant and the parts thereof to be used to derive maximum benefit. If you go through homeopathic medicines, you will find most of the medicines prepared with extracts (tinctures) of many plants and herbs, and various dilutions are prepared after the juices of plants, have been extracted. For an effective and immediate gains, plants extracts are processed in alcohol and then served to patients in drop doses. Sometimes even material extract of plants is used for still quicker results.

In Ayurveda, herbs are also used in most of the preparations, if not all, either in the form of powder, Asava, Arishtha, decoction, for massaging, for local application etc. In fact, herbs are an inseparable part of Homeopathy and Ayurveda.

2

Facts About Herbs

AVAILABILITY OF HERBS

Attention of medical world turned away from herbs due to vast researach on Allopathic medicines which have still no equal. There was no research for new Homeopathic herbal medicines. Same was the case in Ayurveda. Necessity is the mother of invention. If there is no demand, there won't be any production which is boosted by demand factor. Due to deforestation in cities, villages, plains and hills and jungles, trees and plants are still being mercilessly felled, despite legal ban in certain specified regions. It has disturbed ecological balance. The smokes emitted by thermal power houses, factories, quarries, and toxic chemicals released into air and already depleting water resources have vitiated and contaminated environs. We neither get pure water nor fresh and pure air. Earth has been soiled by imprudent and excessive uses of pesticides and chemical manures.

Plants require a fertile soil, seeds, air and water to grow

but when these plant nutrients are vitiated and contamined, either the plants won't grow to full bloom and if at all they grow, their growth will be much below expectations and, their yield will also be fare less. Over and above that, whatever booty we get is neither pure nor toxin-free. Hence, the plants and herbs we get had already lost their medicinal efficacy at the growth stage itself. So, the much sought-after medicinal value seems to be ebbing out of herbs and what we get in return, after hefty expense, is nothing but simply a residual semblance of herbs. In short, herbs mostly, and used that too in good condition and quality, are not easy to get

GROWING AND BUYING OF HERBS

Buying Herbal Plants

All the herbs cannot be grown in all the seasons and many herbs grow and flourish under particular climatic condition, soil. While buying plants ensure that—

1. Herbs are purchased from a reliable Nursery.
2. Price are reasonable and not exorbitant.
3. If plants are bought in later part of spring, nurseries have planty of healthy and young plants which are free from danger of frosts.
4. Specimen of plants should be healthy and strong, and there must be plenty of space in the pot to help the young plants grow.
5. Do not purchase herbs which are yellow or withered, or even straggling. Loose soil points to recent replanting.
6. Make sure that the underside portion of herbs is free from pests such as whitefly, red spider mite and aphids.
7. Finally check that the plants are properly and correctly labelled, as chances of mistake are always present.

GROWING THE PLANTS

Herbal plants can be easily grown in gardens or window

boxes. Annual and benial herbs should be sown at the soil where they are intended to be grown. In this respect closely follow the instructions on the container/packets. The herbs which can be sown easily and that grow also easily are Chamomile Dill, Pot Marigold. Perrenial herbs which grow well from seeds are fennel, elecampane, hyssop, thyme, fever few, ribwort plantain and skull cap, sage, dandelion, white decidnettle and chickweed grow as weeds.

Divide roots with a mine fork/sharp spade, and replant immediately but don't forget to water properly and throughly. Pepperment, Chamomile, (Roman), and Elecampane could be propagated by cutting and replanting small offsets and runners. These herbs should be planted in early spring.

Woody perrenial herbs, like sage, rosemerry, hyssop, lavender thyme are best propagated by cuttings taken from side shoots either in early autumn or late simmer. base of the root should be dipped in hormone rooting powder and pot.

How to Dry Herbs

Availability of fresh herbs is restricted by seasonal growing patterns of herbs. Hence, it is better to store such herbs which are not available all the year round. These herbs should be (1) gathered (2) dried (under shade, and not under sunlight, (3) stored and (4) Preserved under most hygienic conditions lest their efficacy and utility is reduced.

USEFUL POINTS FOR STORING AND DRYING OF HERBS

(i) Herbs should be tried as quick as possible under natural shade, but protected from direct sunlight in any case otherwise the direct sunlight will divest the herbs from natural and valuable aromatic constituents.

(ii) Herbs will try quickly at place where plenty of fresh air is available and, thus will not deteriorate due to oxidation.

(iii) Never dry herbs in a garage, as petrol fumes are liable to contaminate them.

(iv) Use a dry garden-shed, aventilated and airy cupboard, an airy and sunny room, using a low-powered fan for drying purpose, keeping room temperature from 70°-90°F.

(v) If the drying process takes more than a week, the herbs are most likely to lose flavour and get discoloured.

(vi) If herbs are dried in microwave ovens, their chemical composition (s) will get altered.

DRYING OF AERIAL PARTS & LEAVES

Prepare small bunches of herbs – that is leaves and aerial parts – and hang them through a clip, thread, or any other method on some wire, rope, after binding them tightly. When they dry up, crumble their leaves (including small pieces), if so required. If the stems have small seeds and/or flowers, hang them in small bunches and see that they are fully covered with paper bag(s) so that small leaves and seeds that do not fall on ground, rather those remain contained and preserved in the bag itself. This method will, invariably, apply to lavender or dill and all other such varieties that support seeds and small flowers.

Herbs, like pot marigold, have large flowers. Such herbs should be first cut from stems and dried thereafter in trays/in cupboards where air can gain entry – but no dust or direct sunlight should be let in, otherwise medicinal value of the herbs will be lost.

Wash the roots of herbs with thorough perfection and clean them so that any dust, mud adhering to the same gets removed. Roots should always be pulled out when they are fresh. After having done, as advised, chop the root into small pieces which should be spread evenly on a tray in a cooling oven or an airing cupboard.

Garlic and onion are bulbar vegetables, whose round stem or shoot remain ingrained in the earth, should be collected during season when their aerial roots have died down.

Bark of trees/bushes is an outer sheething cover of plants, and should be carefully removed so as not to cut the stem itself while cutting. Remove only the outer covering. After collecting the bark, adopt the same procedure as suggested under 'roots' above. As for berries, they should be collected only after they have ripened and then dealt with as in case of roots.

BUYING HERBS (DRIED)

Number of medicinal herbs is quite large; hence it is not possible to grow, dry and store them in a kitchen-garden. In order to obviate this problem, only frequently used herbs should be grown in a house-garden and preserved, as detailed above. But, for rest of the varieties, one has to depend on shops selling dried herbs. Certain herbs are extremely costly and, thus, should be bought as and when required or only a minimal quantity stored at home, simply to meet exigencies. Herbs which are used quite often and also available freely all the year round in dried form should be bought for a week or so. It is no use blocking money and space when availability of herbs is quite easy. Following guidelines may be kept in mind while buying dried herbs from a shop.

(i) Herbal selling shop must be reliable and charge only reasonable rates.

(ii) Herbs can also be obtained from outside (your city, village) vendors who can mail them or send through courier or any other mode of despatch. If herbs are to be imported and it takes time to receive them, it is better to send your indent, well in advance, so that the parcel reaches you prior to your stock-in-hand exhausts. Always take the cushion time in mind.

(iii) When herbs reach you, check up for finest quality thereof, otherwise you may be a loser. If it meets your Criteria, then only store them in pottery jars or dark glass containers.

(iv) Though there is no expiry date, speaking generally, for the herbs, but herbs faded out in colours and waning strong smells are not worth buying. Always ensure that herbs do not lose their aroma and colour.

(v) Quite often, though not always, wrong labels are pasted on the containers. You can easily make out whether the herbs supplied have all the known characteristics (for instance peculiar and known seed pods in the skull cap), smells, aroma, appearance, etc.

(vi) Herbs, which have not be harvested and looked after properly, are liable to become contaminated which must not be purchased.

(vii) You must ensure that there are no (dry) grass roots, other plant material which ought to have been segregated, nor are their signs of moth, insect infestation, mouse dropping or any amount of any foreign matter.

(viii) When the aforesaid criteria are met, the procured herbs should be preserved in jars which are free from moisture, dust, other impurities, and stored away from direct sunlight, but stored in an any place.

3

Healing Power of Herbs

As already indicated, there are a number of herbs which are exclusively used for healing purposes, out of which around 100 herbs are used for the desired purpose. Even now names, action, reaction and side-effects and their utility for removal of human suffering remain masked or exposed remotely. Some of the well known herbs have vanished into oblivion, utility of some herbs was known only to a selected few (persons). Hence most magnificient therapeutic values remained shrouded in mystery.

DISORDERS TREATED/CURED BY HERBAL TREATMENT

1. Cold, flu, chills, Malaria, typhoid, Dengue fever.
2. Hay fever, Catarrh, Epistaxis, Coryza.
3. Respiration and chest problems, including allergies, asthma and tuberculosis.
4. Skin diseases, including allergy-related skin

infestations.

5. Problems relating to women, viz puberty, menstruation, pregnancy, parturition, menopause and female sex problems.
6. Venereal diseases and urinary disorders.
7. Digestion related diseases, including those of liver, spleen, pancreas, intestines, anus, rectum & stomach.
8. Eye and Ear Problems.
9. Nervous disorders, sleeplessness.
10. Pains and aches, including neuralgias of various eteologies, Headache, Migraine, Bell's Palsy, Neuritis etc.
11. Diseases of Mouth, Throat, including larynx, pharynx, tongue, uvula, soft palate, fauces.
12. Senile and decay of growing age.
13. Disease of infants, children, adolescents, young persons, including their sex related problems; growth problems.
14. Disease of generative and reproductive organs.
15. Psychic upsets.
16. Disease of bones, joints and soft tissue, including accidents/trauma.

Above-mentioned diseases and areas of manifestation are simply an indication as to broad fold of herbal treatment applicability. It would a hyperbolic claim if one asserts authoritatively that herbs could treat each and every disorder with which a person is likely to suffer. No! it is simply belying the truth. Frankly speaking, no established or alternate system can boast of curing all the diseases. If that was so simple and easy, only one system of medicine was enough. But (tall) claims and actual achievements are two polls apart. Success rate in many diseases is still apallingly low, and herbal treatment is no exception to such a dismal spectrum. To my mind, all systems are supplementary to each other, and excellence in certain fields simply bears testimony about the limitations and success rate about a particular system. If one system, excels in a particular field, the other fails or is not so successful and it is true the other way round also. To sum up, no single system of medicine is perfect in itself nor should it ever boast of the same.

CLASSIFICATION OF HERBS

It is pointed out that all herb plantations, growing over the globe, do not posess medicinal properties and applications. Further, certain herbs are to be avoided as their therapeutic values and properties have yet to be probed and discovered. Hence selective, judicious use of herbs is the basic requisite.

PROMINENT (KEY) MEDICINAL HERBS

Agrimony

Pot Marigold

Marshmallow

Yarrow

St. John's Wort

Meadoswseet

Lavender

Rosemerry

Chamomile

Wood Betony

Thyme

Vervain

Note : These are selected key herbs often used to dispel certain specific disorders and their applications are multifold which will be described later on.

KITCHEN REMEDIES

Fennel	Cinnamon
Lemon	Tea
Onion	Cabbage

Garlic

Nutmeg

OTHER USEFUL HERBS

Boneset	Celery
Hops	Burdock
Liquorice	Garlic (Repeated)
Hyssop	Plantain
Eucalyptus	Ishaghula
Echinacea	Raspberry
Elecampane	Lemon Balm
White Deadnettle	Peppermint
Sage	Yellow Dock
Elder	Dandelion
Heartsease	Ginger
Valerian	Skull Cap

HERBS HAVING TONIC EFFECT

Gotu Kola (Indian Pennywort)

Korean Ginseng

Siberian Ginsengh

Dang Kui (Chinese Angelica)

Damiana

Reishi (Ling Zhi)

Asparagus Racemosus (Shatavari)

Withania Somnefera (Ashwagandha)

Mucuna Pruriens (Kaunch-ke-Beej)

Dioscorea (Varahikand Bulbifera)

MISCELLANEOUS HERBS OFTEN USED IN MEDICINAL PREPARATIONS

Alfalfa
Aniseed
Asafoetida
Babul/Keekar
Bael fruit
Banyan
Bellaric Myrobalan
Betel
Bishop's Weed
Black Nightshade
Butea
Caraway Seeds
Cardamom
Cassia
Castor
Celery
Chebulic Myroblan
Chicory
Cinnamon
Coriander
Clove
Curry leaves
Dandelion
Datura
Indian Hemp
Indian Pennywort
Indian Sorrel
Indian spikenard
Kantakari
Medhuca
Margosa
Parsley
Pipal (Peepal)
Poppy seeds
Rauwolfia
Rhubarb
Rough chaff
Sandalwood
Saussurea
Tamarind
Trailing Eclipta
Turpeth
Vasaka
Watercress
Winter Cherry
Wood apple
Rosemerry
Indian Mallow

Following herbs are also used in medicines but are not given much prominence, for unknown reasons, though they form essential part in preparation of various indigenous medicinal combinations.

Dill
Ephendra
Fenugreek
Henna
Holy Basil
Indian Gooseberry
Colchicum
Devil's Tree
Digitalis
East Indian Roseberry
Euphoria
Fennel
Goolar
Gokulakanta
Hermal
Hyssop
Indian Acalypha
Indian Aloe
Indian Berry
Indian Mallow
Valerian
Zizyphus

Ashoka
Bay Berry
Bloodwort
Calamus
Chalmogra
Chirayata
Indian Podophyllum
Indian Sarasaparilla
Indian Squill
Jaundice Berry
Lemon Balm
Lemon Grass
Linseed
Marigold
Marjoram
Parslane
Pergularia
Picorhiza
Saffron
Snake Gourd
Tenner's Cassia
Wormwood

History of Herbs

(4)

Most of the names amongst the herbs listed above are well known to most of us. Not only that, most of them are being rather frequently used to offset effects of common ailments. In our country certain fruits, vegetables and herbs are offered as oblation to deities also. Attaching certain vegetations to some deities enhances their religious importance. Not only that, herbs were used to counteract and offset evil effects of witchcraft and evil spirits.

Curative properties of herbs are not new to our countrymen, and their use has been in vogue since the time of *'Ramayana'*. Fairly detailed account of herbs can be found in *Atharvaveda*, though there are scattered references in *Rigveda* and also *Sushruta* and *Charaka Samhitas* are replete with description and curative potential of over hundred seven herbs – a few of which do not exist in India. Blending of cultures and exchange/ migration of population brought in view more that 500 herbs. Chinese have introduced about 1000 herbs whose description dates back to 2800 B.C. Father of modern medicine Hippocrates

(A Greek physician) also listed hundreds of herbal varieties all, taken together suffice to prove and establish the significance, importance and usage of herbs as a means to cure various diseases.

In India M/s R.N.Chopra, Kirtikar, Basu, Dutt, Mukherjee, Editors of 'Wealth of India' and many other enthusiasts and reearchers have done yeoman's service by their hard work. They have compiled, researched and arranged valuable information, data, details on various plants and herbs which have inherent and proven medicinal curative values. Development of herbal medicine owes a lot to Indian, Chinese, Eygptian, Greek, Tibetan systems of medicine. European countries are late entrants in the field of herbal medicine. William Turmor (1476), William Turmer (1551), John Gerard (1545), John Parkinson (1640), Nicholos Culpeper (1649), William Coles (17th Century). In the later part of 17th Century discovery of 'New Science' almost brought a revolution in the realm of herbal medicine. The Credit for dissemination of herbal knowledge actually took an upward swing after the First World War, when acute shortage of synthesised drugs compelled the medical experts to look to herbal treatment as an effective alternate treatment. Wide acceptance of herbs and herbal medicines is a pointer to the fact that herbs have starting replacing even the most popular therapies–if not fully at least partly.

Common man is baffled by repeated incidence of drug reactions and drug-interactions, plenty of Dos-and-Dont's. It is no use taking a medicine that, instead of curing the basic malady, creates its own (horrible) symptoms or else a new disorder. Herbs have least side-effects but they are neither infallible nor a panacea. There are still wonders in herbs which act magically and can be termed as 'Palliatives' or 'Soothers' or 'Tranquilisers' or 'Mood stabilizers'. People have been so much fascinated and impressed by curing power of herbs that they have made them an almost inseparable part of their 'Kitchen Garden' and 'Home Garden'.

At the age of 73, John Parkinson's 'Theatrum Botanicum' was published in 1640, in which he gave lengthy details of over 3800 plants. But much work still needs to be done in herbal field. There are still vast avenues and opportunities which, if captured, will go a long way in mitigating suffering of vast multitude. In India, there are renowned firms which exclusively process medicines, syrups, tea, decoction, linctus, creams, lotions, beauty-aids, Hair-care aids, oil extracts, geriatic and aphrodisiac drugs from plants and herbs. There are still untapped virgin areas which need to be probed and researched.

Parts of Herbs used in Medicines and Various Uses

(5)

Stem
Root
Rind
Leaves-Dried or Fresh
Flowers/Petals
Fresh/Dried Aerial Parts

There are variable properties (of medicinal values) in each part of plant, hence use of a particular part will be determined in relation to its use in a specific disorder.

For instance, lemon fruit, juice stem, leaves and rind are used for various applications and this rule applies to all other herbs and plants.

WAYS TO USE HERBS

Certain herbs have tough rind & root which cannot be reduced to powder forms whereas others are to be used in the form of infusions, Decoctions, oils, Pills/Tablets or else filled in capsules, or used simply in powdered form. Tinture is also extracted from some herbs. Other forms being juices, syrups, creams, ointments, liniments, essential oils, infusions/tea bags. To sum up, herbs can be used in the form of :

1. Infusions / Teabags
2. Combination of decoction/infusion
3. Hot infused oils
4. Cold infused oils
5. Pills and Tablets
6. Capsules
7. Tinctures
8. Syrups and Juices
9. Creams and Ointments
10. Essential Oils
11. Poultices

Purpose of converting various parts of plants into above-mentioned forms is to make the final preparation more patient friendly. For instance powder, pills or tablets cannot be gulped down by infants, children, pregnant ladies and aged persons who can easily take syrups, linctus, sweetened decoctions, teas and infusions. Moreover, any medicine taken in liquid/paste forms instantly metabolises and thus, induces quicker effect, whereas Tablets and Pills take longer to metabolise and are a bit difficult to swallow. Hence, herbal preparations are prepared in such a way that they satisfy requirement of various age-groups and sexes.

If a patient is averse to taking pills or tablets, it is better to dissolve them in water or any other permissible Vehicle so as to make the same more acceptable to the patient.

Methods of Converting Herbs to Various Forms
Infusions :

Herbal infusions can be taken cold or hot (in the same manner as tea beverage is taken) by adding some sugar, honey or/and, in some cases, salt also.

You need flowers, fresh/dried herbs, host of aerial parts, seeds etc. Take a kettle or tea pot which should have tight lid. First put in 75 gms of fresh herbs or 25 gms of dried herbs and pour 500 ml hot water over the ingredients or simply let the two be mixed in a kettle and closed with a lid which should be tight enough so as not to let out steam. The contents should remain in the container for 10-15 minutes whereafter the infusion should be strained into a cup by using a strainer. Rest of the quantity may be stored in fridge or cool place. Preparation should be processed to last for 24 hours so that 3-4 doses could be taken daily. So much so for a day's consumption.

If fresh infusion is required/desired, then put 2 TSP of herbs (dried) into the strainer and pour fully boiled water over it, and cover with a lid. Let it infuse for ten minutes and then, after removing the strainer, use it. These cups are called as 'Tisane cups' which are not difficult to procure.

Tea-Bags

As preparing infusions first and then storing in a cool place may seem, to some persons an arduous take, they can use herbal teabags (processed by means of specific herbs for use in particular use/disorder) in the same way as ordinary tea bags are used to prepare a cup of tea. If herbal tea bags are neither handy nor available, then put in 1-2 TSP of dried herbs in a piece of fine cloth (say Muslin) and tie the same with thread, leaving enough margin at the top to hold the cloth. Let it infuse in a cup of tea for 10-15 minutes in boiled water. Lastly, if the herbs are available in powder (pulverised) form, then add 30 gms of powdered herbs to 500ml hot water–stir with a spoon and drink hot cup, the rest may be stored in a cool place.

I am of the view that each time fresh infusion should be prepared and taken fresh or according to requirement. Herbal teas are not now delight and privilege of the elite and rich class, they can be used even by a common man earning average income or else the herbal powder can be easily processed at home–it will ensure fresh ingredients at much lower cost.

Decoctions

In Ayurveda decoctions are known as 'Quaths' certain plants have tougher part which, in order to extract their optimum healing properties and other constituents, are required to be decocted/simmered, though it is often said that heating or boiling/simmering a plant takes away its medicinal properties. In order to preserve its quality, process of maceration (i.e. softening the plant by soaking in water.) may be adopted but, it is a fact that certain plants remain tough and hard despite being macerated; hence the need to decoct.

For purposes of decoction, dried/fresh berries, roots, seeds and bark are used. No aluminium utensil must ever be used for decocting a plant or any part thereof, instead use enamel, ceramic, glass, stainless steel or fireproof pottery; nylon or plastic sieve for straining purposes and a jug with a tight lid.

General ratio between fresh herbs and water should not exceed 1:30; i.e. If you take 25 gms of herbs, only 750ml water should be added thereto. If more than one herb is required to be used then the ratio should be 1:25. After simmering, residual water content should be stand reduced to 2/3rd (500ml) quantity. The final quantity, so processed, should last for a whole day, and should be preserved, after being strained, in a jug having a lid for covering it, in a cool place.

Normal or standard dose being 150-175 ml (or a cup of tea or a wineglass) – to be taken thrice a day. The suggested quantity and frequency of dose may be varied and moderated according to status and stage of the disease. Add lemon juice or a little honey to improve flavour.

Process of Preperation

Put in suggested quantity of herb(s) and water in a sauce pan of stainless steel and let it simmer for 25-45 minutes or till the contents come to a boiling point and quantity is reduced to 2/3rd of total contents. It is better if heat is kept at low/ medium level. Now strain the residual contents through a sieve. After taking the first dose, store the surplus quantity into a jug and preserve (covered with a lid) the same at a cool place or in a fridge at normal temperature; but not to freezing point, in any case.

Blending of Infusion & Decoction

Method of combining infusions/decoctions is intended to combine qualities of flowers, leaves, barks, roots and berries, so as to derive optimum medicinal benefits and that too with quicker and better results. Quantity of the recipes will remain the same as indicated earlier.

Take a saucepan and fill it with 750 ml of cold water and put in roots/bark and berries, and cover the pan with a lid. Let the contents simmer until it is reduced to 2/3rd quantity. Now take a jug (with lid) or a teapot and put in leaves/dried flowers into it. Next step is to strain the decoction on to the dried herbs in the jug/tea-pot and allow to infuse for 10-15 minutes. Finally, strain the combined decocted and infused stuff into a cup. If taste permits, add some honey/unrefined sugar and sip hot. Dosage and frequency will depend upon the intensity and gravity of disorder but, in any case, there must be a gap of 6 hours between each dose (i.e. in all three doses should be taken and not beyond that). It is better to take the mixture hot which should be prepared fresh each time.

Infused Oils

Infused oils are utilised for rubbing and massaging purposes on head, forehead, chest, neck, shoulders etc to ward off aches and pains, for general massage, for inducing sleep, to calm down and pacify agitated nerves.

Roots, aerial parts and dried leaves are used for the processing purposes. Equipment required consists of saucepan, glass bowl/double saucepan, a muslin bag and wine press/Jelly bag, large-sized jug; fully sterilized and airtight bottle(s) (Funnel is optional).

Put 500 ml of sunflower oil to 200 gms of fully dried herb(s) – all should be put in and stored in dark glass bottles and kept in a cool place — away from direct sunlight – and allowed to stay for a year. The bottle should be filled to its 2/3rd capacity. Occasionally stir the bottle, making sure that the bottle is securely tightened with a cork or lid-cover.

Hot Infused Oils

Other method is to put the contents of herb and oil into top part of double saucepan/glass bowl– the lower part being filled with water (which may be required to be filled again). Now simmer the contents for about 3 hours. After it has been boiled on slow/medium fire, the liquified content should be strained by means of a jelly bag/wine press and let the contents fall into a jug. Finally, store the contents in glass bottles of dark colour, and rest of the procedure to be followed has been detailed under 'infused oil' above.

Mostly used hot infused oils can be used for pains and aches (by Rosemary oil); arthritis, bruises and sprains (by hot oil, prepared from dried leaves of (comfrey) and irritant eczema (by hot oil of dried aerial parts of chickweed).

Cold Infused Oils

Equipments to be used are the same as detailed under 'Hot infused oils'. Here, only dried petals and flowers are to be used. Put the herbs in a jar and put in oil, in sufficient quantity, of safflower, walnut or sunflower oil. Now, pack and seal the jar and tightly cover with a lid (preferably a threaded lid/cover) and let it remain on a sunny window for two weeks at least.

After exposure for the said period, pour the mixture in a jelly bag/wine press, so as to extract the oil. The extracted oil should be bottled in a dark glass bottles and stored in a cool place.

Cold oil extracted out of fresh/dried petals of Pot Marigold can be used for disorders like thrush, athlete's foot, grazes etc. But for burns and minor scalds, sunburn, grazes and inflamed joints oil, prepared from fresh flowering tops of St.John's Wort should be used.

Tablets & Pills

Due to technological advance and keeping in mind variable and nauseating tastes of people, most of the companies process sugar-coated pills/tablets for which they use milk sugar (lactose) as a base. Certain persons, being allergic to milk or to other milk products, avoid taking pills. In order to obviate this problem, sugar is used (not milk sugar) for the purpose. Certain companies present pills/tablets in an enteric coated form which are resistant to stomach acid, thus preventing their dissolution until they reach the lower bowels. This method avoids stomach irritation. Normally a tablet contains 500-600 mg contents of ingredient(s) of dried herb.

Capsules

Capsules are made of giletin which can stick anywhere in the food passage if taken without water or any other Vehicle: Herb powder is stored in a capsule to the extent of 600 mg (per capsule) which could be a single entity or combination of other herbal powders. If not wrapped in air-tight packages, capsules can be distorted under damp weather conditions. Those, who dislike capsules, should take pills/tablets instead, and it applies in reverse order also. If some medicine (herbal) is available in capsule form only and patient despises its use, he should separate the gelatin portion and take the powder with some water or honey.

Tinctures

Herbal tinctures are obtained by soaking herbal extracts in water and alcohols and then brew is pressed to get a liquid, the colour of which is either dark green or brown. Many herbal extracts can be mixed together.

To get 25% resultant water, mixture or alcohol, 100 gms of dried herb/herbs should be placed in a big jar which should

41

be big enough to accommodate 165 ml water and 335 ml Vodka (of 37.5% potential). This mixture is to be retained in a jar, having a screwed top, and kept under sun/shade for about 15 days, but shaken/stirred almost once daily. After the said period, use a muslin jelly bag or wine press to strain the mixture which should be retained and stored in a clean bottle of glass. Normal dose is 1TSP (5ml) thrice daily. This mixture (tincture) can be safely retained for a period of two years, if protected properly.

Syrups

These are generally palatable and easier to take than tablets/pills/capsules, due to their sweetened taste. Generally syrups are used for coughs and inflammed throat conditions, or in the form of tonics or as Vehicles (as used with Ayurvedic medicines). Sugar is the excipient that is used for preparing herbal syrups. Herbal extracts are used for processing syrups such as from hyssop, liquorice, marshmellow, elecampane, thyme etc, as also from potent expectorants like squills and Ipecacuanha. General (adult) dose is from 5-10 ml thrice daily.

Juices

Juices of herbs are extracted from herbs, like oats, chamomile, dandaleon onion, lemon balm, St.John's Wort, Rosemary, Valerian, Thyme, Yarrow etc. Herbal juices can be taken independently or combined with tinctures. Certain herbal juices are not palatable; hence some honey/sugar to taste may be added thereto. If a bottle of juice has been opened, the same should be placed in a fridge. It is, however, better to prepare fresh juices, as and when required.

Creams And Ointments

Creams get easily absorbed. They soften the skin due to use of fats, oils and water-based ingredients/substances. Certain creams contain mixture of petroleum-derived bases and organic fats, and preservatives are added to enhance and improve shelf-life. There are certain creams which are 'Cold' and 'Vanishing'—the former used in cold and the other in summer season.

Ointments Contain : Oils and fats, parrafin, wax or petroleum jelly. Since there is no amount of water in ointments, they keep the skin moist and soft and stay longer on the skin–the reason being that they form a protective layer over the skin. Any part of the body which remains in contact with moisture requires application of ointment. They contain natural oils, fats and linoleum, According to state of disease and requirement either of the local applications can be used.

Certain useful creams and ointments prepared from some herbs are as follows:

(i) **Chamomile :** For allergic skin infections and eczema.

(ii) **Arnica :** For chilblains, sprains, bruises and swelling due to some trauma (Do not use if the skin is broken or bleeding).

(iii) **Chickweed :** Is useful to draw out splinters, corns or boils. Also efficacious in irritant eczema.

(iv) **Comfrey :** For sprains and bruises (if skin is not broken) and in arthritic conditions.

(v) **Evening Primrose :** For eczema and dry skin.

(vi) **Pot Marigold :** Fungal infections, dry eczema, cuts, and grazes.

(vii) **Heartsease :** For skin rashes and Nappy Rash (particularly in infants).

(viii) **Sage :** It is used as a first-aid cream as it is a general antiseptic cream. Useful also in insect stings.

(ix) **Slippery Elm :** Used for corns and splinters as a drawing ointment.

(x) **Witch Hazel :** It is an astringent and used for Vericose Veins and piles.

(xi) **Elderflower :** Useful in Chapped hands.

(xii) **Tea Tree :** For fungal infections, such as thrush, as an antiseptic cream.

Essential Oils

They are highly concentrated extracts of herbs and are most effective even if used in 2-4 drops. These are added to sweet almond oil, wheatgerm oil sunflower oil and other vegetable oils or 1-2 drops dropped into bathing water (say 5-6 drops of essential oil). No essential oil should be used or applied over skin, inserted into nose, ears or eyes, mouth; other orifices of body, as they are skin irritants and cause immense damage, but may be diluted with water/oil; or infused herbal oil, or massaged, but after being mixed with oils). one or two drops may be added (of an essential oil) to two nil of carrier oil.

Essential oils are also used in aromatherapy (in diluted form only) in form of tonics, and as relaxants; to remove aches and pains, for skin care, to induce sleep, to act as aphrodisiac and finally to create ambience.

Following essential oils may be diluted with appropriate oils to get relief, calmness and aromatic flavour.

Rose Oil : It is the most delicious and costliest oil and is king among oils.

Sweet Basil : It is particularly good for doing away with respiratory disorders and complications and also acts as a general restorative.

Fennel : It is used mostly for digestive disorders.

Lemon Balm : Used to cheer up tired hearts and minds, also as 'Pick-me-up' device. It enlivens and cheers up spirits and is a great 'mood booster'.

Sweet Marjoram : It is quite often used for soothing pains and aches, strains and bruises.

Aromatic Aphrodisiacs : Ylang Ylang tops the list of aphrodisiac oils and all other oils are just secondary to it.

Aromatic Ambience : Use Patchouli, benzoin and Ylang

Ylang oils or citrus oils like that of grapefruit, or sandalwood oil for the purpose.

Liquorice : It is of unquestioned value in treating arthritis, coughs and ulcers but must be used moderately so as not to have any side-effect and/or reaction.

A. Gardiner describes following 'Top Ten Oils', viz, Oil of :

Top Ten Oils

1. Cypress
2. Chamomila.
3. Eucalyptus
4. Geranium
5. Juniper
6. Lavender
7. Sandalwood
8. Rosemary
9. Ylang Ylang, and lastly
10. Ti Tree or Tea Tree

Secondary Oils

1. Basil
2. Benzoin
3. Bergamot
4. Black Pepper
5. Cajaput or Cajeput
6. Cedarwood-B
7. Citronella
8. Clergy Sage
9. Fennel
10. Frankin Cense
11. Ginger

12. Grapefruit
13. Lemon
14. Lemon grass
15. Marjoram
16. Lemon Balm or Melissa
17. Myrrh
18. Orange Blossom or Neroli
19. Niaouli
20. Orange, sweet
21. Palmarosa
22. Patchouli
23. Peppermint
24. Petigrain
25. Roseweed
26. Tangerine, and
27. VetiVert

A. Gardiner has listed 37 top and secondary herbs from which oil is extracted/processed for various therapeutic applications but there is another list of vegetable oils which have both food and medicinal values but, all said **and** done, the aforesaid list of herbs would suffice to meet our purpose, even though some of the herbs are either not easily available or are simply imported. Mustard, Coconut, Linseed, Sandalwood, Castor seeds, Cinnamon, Soyabeen, Clove, etc-are still rampantly used in kitchen and medicines.

Preparing a Poultice

Poultice is used for fomentation. Main purpose behind preparing and applying the poultice (which is a preperation of hot moist material) to any part of the body is to alleviate pain, increase circulation of blood locally or soften the skin to allow the matter to be expressed from a boil. Fresh plants/herbs can be directly by applied to injuries or ailing sites.

To prepare a poulitce, chop the herb into small pieces and boil for about five minutes. After this, sequeeze any surplus liquid out. Spread or apply oil on the affected part so that the part is smooth and material does not stick. Then spread the herb mixture on the affected part, and secure it (pultice) with gauze/cotton strips. Let if remain there for 2-4 hours whereafter it can be reapplied fresh.

It is once again repeated, each herb has its own therapeutic values and varied uses; hence no herb should be used, in any form, quantity or shape, indiscreetly, without knowing the healing power and probable reactions. Certain herbs are so dangerously harmful that they can create health problems also. Always seek advice of a herbalist in so far as dosage, mode of application/usage is concerned. If you act otherwise, you will simply be landing yourself or your patient into worse situation. In Ayurveda effect of each herb changes when a Vehicle is changed. That is change of Vehicle can improve/worsen the disease. If some reaction sets in, the same can be reversed by simply substituting one vehicle with another. It is so simple but, without proper knowledge, nothing can work out to your advantage.

6

Herbalism

Herbalism seeks to restore body's Vital force or 'Self-healing mechanism' or else to fortify the depleted body forces so as to activate them to such an extent that the body is in a position to combat any disease. Herbalism is a holistic medical system that prescribes medicines, keeping in view not only patient's symptoms but also taking into account the actual cause of illness, dietary standard, his living pattern or unhealthy lifestyle or excessive stress which, when combined together, over-burden patient's (delicate) balance and surface in the form of disease/illness.

Herbalists attribute cause of a disease to body's symptoms but also taking into account the actual cause of illness, dietary standard, his living pattern or unhealthy lifestyle or excessive stress which, when combined together, over-burden patient's (delicate) balance and surface in the form of disease/illness.

Herbalists attribute cause of a disease to body's disharmony, that is 'Homeostatis'. Hence a herbalist will treat the patient as a whole, but never in isolation. He will prescribe only such remedies as are capable of promoting healing by restoring homeostatis. The herbalist is supposed to have complete knowledge as to which part of a plant is to be used and in which condition. He should also know which symptoms a herb can ameliorate or aggravate. In medical herbalism, 'herbal synergy' is a key factor. According to this theory a plant should be used as a whole and not its isolated constituents — the latter being used in synthetically processed drugs. Herein lies the major difference in approach between pharmacentical drugs based on isolated extracts of plants and herbal medicines.

If all parts of a plant are used in medicines, therapeutic effect of ingredients will be greater and quicker, and totality of effects will enhance which advantages are not available when an isolated ingredient of a plant is used.

Most pharmaceutical concerns isolate and synthesize active ingredients of plants. For instance, Meadow sweat plant is used to treat digestion related disorders but it contains salicylic acid (which is basis of Aspirin drug) which (Aspirin) can upset digestion and also cause internal bleeding in persons who have sensitive stomach (mucus) lining.

In order to gain entry into U.S.A., Europe and Australia, a herb must be backed by confirmed positive research findings. Clinical research has, however, confirmed therapeutic uses of herbs like, Ginger, Gingke, Garlic, St.John's Wort and Echinacea. To quote an example, Maharshi Ayurveda's cholesterol lowering medicine 'Amrita Kalash' took plenty of time to get approval, acceptance and marketing permission in the U.S.A. But, it is a fact that all herbal medicines need to be backed by scientific evidence to get recognition and permission for sale.

WESTERN HERBALISM

I have already explained earlier the forms in which herbs are used in the Western World viz Decoctions, Infusions, infused oils, Tinctures, creams, ointments, poultices etc which are generally preserved in the form of tablet, pill, tincture, essential oil. Method of processing and testing various toxic and curative properties of Herbs is more precise, voluminous, dependable, trustworthy, coming as it does from standard and reputed testing laboratories. Herbs are mixed with other medicinal ingredients to derive more effective and quicker results. There are certain herbal experts who have their own dispensaries where they prepare medicines to suit an individual patient's need. In order to widen the field of Herbs, plant species have been imported from Africa, Australia, North America, Asia to enrich treasure of Herbs which have now become part & parcel of Western Herbalism. Research is an on-going and unending process which still can unravel many more scintillating facts of Herbs. Western Herbalism has still to depend largely on traditional knowledge of Herbs to cure and treat certain diseases. Earlier, the westerners had to contend themselves by the traditional knowledge gained from other countries and regions. Herbal medicine is a new field for the Western World but chances of making breakthrough are still available.

In 1985, W.H.O. commended the role of herbal remedies and confirmed that herbal remedies could fulfil an important role in modern healthcare. The system is now quite well established in continental Europe and an aspirant can study this subject at the U.K.'s Universities. The U.S.A. has also relaxed its law to let in herbal medicines.

CHINESE HERABALISM

This unique system owes its origin as far back as 200 B.C. to 100 A.D. The system is called Traditional Chinese Medicine (TCM). Ideas of harmony, balance and moderation are unique traits of TCM. Further concepts of 'holism' (of Yin and Yang) and the 'five elements' are the three basic foundations of TCM which views the body as a whole single unit. For instance, if one part of body is ailing, entire body has to bear the impact thereof. Hence, when a particular problem of health is solved, it affects the body as a whole through which 'meridians' run – a network of channels carrying 'Vital force' or 'Energy'. All

50

the body organs are fortified, activated and nourished by 'Vital substances' (qi, blood body fluids and "kidney essences", that govern the sexuality, growth and general (body's) constitution of each person. There are two opposing forces in nature—Yin ("Moon" or "overcast") and YANG ('Sun' or 'Sunshine') though looking opposite to each other, are actually complementary in/ of nature. Body becomes diseased, disturbed and emotionally upset when Yin and Yang get disturbed or either of these becomes excessive. The chinese believe that other factors that disturb balances in the body (to surface in the form of disease(s)) include poor diet, pollution, season and weather conditions, emotional disturbances.

TCM is far near to Indian system of medicine (Ayurveda). The mechansim of Yin and Yang can be divided further into – interior, exterior, deficiency, excess, cold and hot – which are three pairs of opposite states. Further, 5 Principles, viz earth, fire, water and wood, and all these five elements can be ascribed to body and nature, because it is the nature which exerts great effect on the body. These five elements are almost akin to five elements of Indian system of medicine and diagnosis. For instance, one element either inhibits or supports the other element, so one organ is affected by less/more functioning of another organ. Fire is douched by water, but fire melts metal, the kidneys (water) control the heart (fire), and heart controls the lungs (metal).

Herbal medicines are used as potent tools to rebalance these five elements and when that goal is achieved, a healthy state of body & mind sets in. Each one of the said five elements denote a specific taste which has been classified as sour, sweet, salty, pungent and bitter. Every herb is claimed to work on (affect) particular organs and meridians, alongwith "Tendencies of actions", ascending and descending, floating and sinking. For instance, a herb endowed with the quality of an 'upward' action would be used to treat a "sinking" disorder like diarrhoea and a "cold" herb (like Huang quin or Baical Skull cap) would be used to bring down 'hot' condition (say high temperature). The approach is to treat a symptom by a herb having the opposite action/quality.

In the Western world, clinical trials have been carried out but the trend towards TCM is not encouraging. Only the herb curing Atopic eczema has found favour with the westerners who are sceptically scared of hazardous side-effects of Chinese herbs. They also do not readily accept and subscribe to concepts of Yin, Yang and qui.

It is very rarely that a simple herb is prescribed for some disorder. A standard formula or prescription, for each disease, has been worked out (with need-based marginal adjustments) that usually contains 10-15 or even more herbs. Each formulation has been worked out in relation to taste, role and temperature. Herbs are prescribed in the form of tablets/pills, pastes, powders, decoctions, lotions, ointments creams, depending on a patient's constitution, age, temperament and pattern of harmony.

There nearly 6000 herbs, a few animal components, minerals, hundreds of standard formulations to choose from and the detailed version of all the herbs is available in 'Traditional Chinese Pharmacopoeia' which includes dried leaves, dreed leaves, dried roots. Tea-bags are easily available, apart from herbs.

Guidelines & Precautions required while using or opting for Chinese Herbs

1. Do not resort to self-medication, especially if you are a pregnant women, infirm, invalid and, old person.
2. Do not go after branded preparations, instead consult a practitioner.
3. Consult your doctor if you have Hepatitis or any other liver problem.
4. Chinese herbal, though said to be quite safe, can have, at times, serious reactions and side-effects.

5. Most of the Chinese medicines taste bitter; hence do not expect any sweet taste.

6. Treatment may take even months, depending on chronicity of the 'disease but 4-6 weeks' period is quite normal. Actual time will depend on the response and pace of recovery. In any case you have to be fair, patient, persevering and reasonable.

7. Allergic reactions cannot be ruled out.

8. Do not expect any magical resutls, though there are herbal medicines/formulations that can and are meant and designed to meet even most emergent situations or crisis stages.

HERBS AND AYURVEDA

Ayurveda is a traditional holistic healing. India system which largely depends on plant support to form major Chunk of its medicines. Most of the herbs, spices, seeds, roots, leaves, rinds and stems, petals and flowers are deeply ingrained in all Indian homes where 'home remedies' are popular. Even certain family members in some family are adept in curing even intricate disorders by simple and cost-effective formulations which, at times, have shown marvellous and astounding results. There is hardly any Indian who does not posess formulas of his own. As an initial step, an attempt is made to first treat the patient with home remedies. If experiences of all such persons are compiled, huge volumes running into thousands of pages could be prepared, though some or quite few of such formulations may be common. People still have an abiding faith in this system which is neither alien/imported. They have been living with this system since centuries. *Basic Ayurvedic tenet that Vegetations, grown on a particular soil in a particular region and climate, are only capable of solving health problems of inmates of that area/region.*

Ayurvedic Principles & Theory

Ether, (Akash), Air (Vayu), Fire (Agni), Water (Jal) and Earth (Prithvi) are the great five elements which underline all living systems. These elements are constantly changing and interacting and can be simplified into three Vitiations (DOSHAS) when these doshas remain under harmony and balance, health of body does not get disturbed but, when their balance gets disturbed, a diseased state sets in.

The three doshas (Humors) are Vata (Wind) Pitta (Bile) and Kapha (Phlegm) and due to predominance of the one humor, a person's personality is determined, that is 'Vata-Prakriti' 'Pitta-Prakriti' or 'Kapha Prakriti', or we can also say that 'Prakriti' is also 'Tendency' of a person. The doshas continue to fluctuate. Each dosha is made of combination of two great elements viz.

1. Vata is formed from ether and air.

2. Pitta is formed from fire and water and

3. Kapha is formed from earth and water

Whether a dosha is predominant or suppressed, can be easily gauged by an adept practitioner, because each individual has quite distinctive attributes/characters which distinguish one person from the other and the recognizable and determining factor/feature being physical form and appearance which depicts his personality/trait and predominance of a dosha. If we compare Chinese and Indian systems of medicines, we will find most features quite common. In a way each person's constitutional frame is a blend of two dominate doshas or else one only which determine his intellectual capacity, physical strength, weaknesses and personality as a whole.

Each dosha has a seat in the body which is able to absorb/ eliminate marginal excesses, thus keeping a dosha within its limitation. Health of a person will depend on the pacification of excesses in the doshas and thus keeping the fluctuations to the bare minimum level will ensure perfect health.

All persons belong to anyone of the 3 tendencies (Prakrittis) such as Sattvik, Rajasik and Tamsik - in descending order of excellence, and these tendencies are hand-and-glove with each other. Moreover, dominance of anyone of doshas and prakritis will determine food habits, character, conduct, behaviour of a person. Weakness and preference for certain food items, or else dislike or abhorance will point out to the specific traits described above.

Types of Persons :

Vata Type

Air is dominant, followed by ether. These persons have tendency to coldness, hence they are nearer to Kapha predominant people. The seat of Vata is Colon. The tastes that increase Vata are pungent, bitter, astringent, hence Vata types should avoid raw foods. Sweet, sour, moist, sally, but warm foods pacify tastes of such people. Hence they prefer cooked root vegetables, casseroles etc. The Vata seasons are early winter and autumn.

These people are of slight, short built, but some of them are tall also. These types are creative, have nervous and quick movements, but are habitual energy wasters. These people can (rather should) take carrots to tone down excess of Vata. Vata exerts greatest influence at dawn. As most of the Vata-related disorders take place on the morning but can be averted or alleviated if medicines are taken at night when cough in the ascendance. If Vata types take medicines on the previous night, they are not likely to suffer from disorder in the following morning.

It is held that about 70-80% diseases are triggered by Vata Dosha.

Pitta Types

Fire is a dominant element, followed by water. Stomach

and small intestines are the seat of this humor. Its quality of lightness is shared by Vata types. Sour, salty, pungent tastes increase pitta; hence they must avoid red meat. But sweet, bitter, astringent, cooling foods (especially salads), fish, Tofu mushrooms, Chicken pacify the tastes of this type of people. Summer is called the Pitta season when it rises in all the foods. Mushrooms pacify most excess of pitta. The hottest part of the day is noon when Pitta is at its zenith.

Persons of Pitta type are of average height, are evenly proportioned, aggressively competitive, ambitious and confident. If noon is the prime time for excess of pitta, middle of night is the secondary pitta period when it rises again.

Kapha Types

Their dominant element is water, followed by earth. Its seat is stomach and lungs, but more so lungs. Oiliness is the shared quality with Pitta. Salty, sweet, sour tastes increase cough; hence cough dominant persons should avoid dairy products. Bitter, astringent, pungent tastes pacify cough, hence they must take spicy and hot foods, pears and apples, beans, lentils and leafy vegetables. Cough is strong in the middle of winter season. Excess of cough is mollified/pacified by apples. Hours, toward midnight, forebode zenith time of cough, and early morning period is the secondary time for cough aggravation.

Kapha type persons are physically strong, inclined to possessiveness, are slow-moving but physically strong and of heavily built.

HERBAL AYURVEDIC MEDICINES

Asavas –(ferment, an intoxicating liquor), Arishtas, Quaths, –(decoction), pastes, chatnies, powders, tablets, pills all contain one part or the other of herbal plants, in variable ratio. In Ayurvedic medicines, all parts of a herbal plant, in one form or the other, are utilized. Certain large and reputed pharmaceutical

Companies have their own plantations of herbs, fruits and vegetables. Anything grown underneath, upon and over the earth is meant for use in Ayurvedic medicines, if it possesses medicinal properties. Even the spices used in Indian homes are an integral part of Ayurvedic pharmacy.

There are about 20 major medicinal herbs which are frequently used in various medicines but no plant, herb, or any part hereof should ever be used without fully knowing therapeutic uses, of side-effects, reactions and incompatability factors. The system has certain 'Magic formulations' which can vie with any such medicine in any therapy (Those who wish to know more about Ayurveda are advised to read Diamond Pocket Book's book entitled 'Ayurvedic Cure for Common Diseases' by the same author). This system is renowned for curing many digestive disorders, including cancerous growths, rheumatism and arthritis, gout and other allied disorders, Asthma, Cough, Tuberculosis, Skin disorders, Viral infections, Hepatitis, Colitis, Heart ailments, Insomnia, Nervous disorders, soft tissue trauma, eye diseases, sight improvement, Anxiety, Insanity, Epilepsy and Menstrual disorders and surprisingly there is hardly any medicine that doesn't contain herbs. Actually, if herbs are deleted from ayurvedic formula preparations, the treasure of ayurveda will be limited only to a few remedies only and same would be the status of Chinese Herbalism.

HERBALISM AND HOMEOPATHY

Except the drugs processed from minerals, metals and animal kingdom, all other medicines are processed from plant extracts which form main chunk of Homeo Materia Medica. For quicker effects most of the mother tinctures contain plant extracts. Since there has been virtually no progress in finding out new remedies, this therapy has to solely depend on what was handed down to it by luminaries like Hahnemann, Clarke, Allen, Boericke, Bonneghausen, Lippe, H.Constantive, Farrington and others. There has not been even semblance of any attempt to break and venture people into new medicines call this system as stagnant, retrograde system. Credit for introducing herbs goes to Indian doctors who took pains to research on some varieties of herbs.

This system also has tablets ointments, creams, mother tinctures made out of herbal extracts. Aloe, Arnica, Bryonia, Belladonna, Aconite, Pulsatilla, Sepia, Echinacea, Ipecac, Jacaranda, ocimum cannum, etc. are some out of long list of Homeo medicines that owe their existence to herbs, plants and their various parts. Vegetable Kingdom is the mainstay of such remedies and there is no denying the fact that there are, no doubt, still 'Magical and wonder drug's in this system which can be compared with any other modern system of medicine, even if such remedies are not many, so to say.

Standard Quantities & Dosages

Infusions

50gm fresh herbs or 25gm dried herbs (or 2 ounces of fresh herbs or 1 ounce of dried herbs), to be added to 500 ml or 16 oz (fluid) or 2 tea cups boiling water. Standard dose being 2/3rd cup (150 ml) or 5 fl.ounces thrice daily. If the infusions are stored in a tightly-stoppered Vessels, they can last for about 3 days, in a fridge.

Decoctions

500 ml/2 cups/16 fl.oz of water for boiling Add.25 gms (1 oz) of dried herbs or 50 gms (2 oz) of fresh herbs to the above-mentioned quantity. After simmering, the fluid contents should stand reduced to 2/3d quantity. Standard dose is 150 ml/2/3 cup/5 fl.oz, to be taken thrice daily. If kept in a fridge, the contents will keep up for 3 days.

Hot Oil Infusons

500 gms/1¼ lb of fresh herbs or 250 gms/9oz of dried herbs added to 500 ml/2 cups/16 fl.oz of pure vegetable oil (viz sunflower oil or sweet almond oil are ideal mediums). In most cases water is also added (say ½ quantity of vegetable oil). Let it simmer until water has fully evaporated. It is a better method when oil doesn't burn, rather water only burns. If only oil is used, the resultant oil should be reduced to ½ the quantity after simmering.

Cold Oil Infusions

The purpose behind processing cold oil infusions is to retain and preserve medicinal properties of plant herbs because medicinal properties of herbs vanish (due to their being volatile) as they escape with heat.

Add 500 gm (1¼ lb) fresh herbs or 250 dried herbs (still better, use herbal powder for quick assimilation in the oil) to 500 ml/2 cups/16 fl.oz of pure vegetable oil. Squeeze out oil after 3 days, but do not expose the contents to direct sunrays.

Tinctures

Take 200 gms dried herb (or 7 oz) or 40 gm (1½ oz) of fresh herb to a litre (4 cups or 1½ PT) 25% alcohol/water mix. For instance, if you are using 40% Vodka, add 375 ml (13 Fl.oz or 1½ cups) or Brandy, water to 600 ml add (2½ cups or 1 PT) spirit to make 25% strength. *Tinctures must* never be given to children and also keep them away from reach of children. Usual and standard adult dose is 1 TSP (5ml), thrice daily diluted with a little water. But dose for concentrated herbs, like ginger, take 10 drops, thrice daily, preferably with water.

Ointments

Add 25 gms (or one ounce) bee-wax to a cup (100 ml, 4fl

oz) of vegetable oil. Add 20-30 drops of essential oil to it. But, if the skin is highly sensitive, use only 10 drops of esential oil.

Creams

25 gms (or 1 ounce) bee wax, 25ml or 5TSP water, and 100ml Vegetable oil. If essential oils are used, then drop 20/30 drops to process medicated cream.

The quantities, mentioned above, are standard quantities which may be altered/modified in accordance with guidance and advice of a herbalist.

8

Use of Herbs in Various Common Disorders

1. Anxiety

Chamonille, Lemon Balm, Lime Blossom Skullcap, Valerian (Valerian officinals).

Oils : Clary Sage, Lavender, Mellessa, Rose and Ylang Ylang.

2. Depression

Gentian, Borage, Oatstraw (Avena Sativa), Rosemarry, Vervain (Verbena officinalis).

Oils : Bergamot, clary sage, Geramum, Neroli.

3. Headache

Chamomile, Lime Blossom, Peppermint, Rosemary

Oils : Peppermint, Lavender, Sandalwood(?)

Sleeplessness (Insomnia)

Chamomile, Hyssop, Lemon Balm, Lime Blossom, Passion flower (Passiflora Incarnata).

Oils : Lavender, Clary Sage, Chamomile, Marjoram.

Hemicrania/Migraine

Chamonile Feverfew, Rosemary.

Oils : Migraine Lavender or Peppermint

4. Neuralgia

Lavender, Flowers, Lime Blossom, ST.John's wort, Vervain (infusion oils of these plants).

Oils : Analgesic oils like oil of Lavender, Rosemary, Chamomile, Marjoram which can be alternated or blended together to yield quicker and better results.

5. Sciatica

Infusions of Chamomile or Lavender to molify and ease inflammation and muscle spasm. Strong decoction of Cramp Bark for acute muscular spasm and using it (herb) as a warm compress.

Oils : Compresses of Lavender or Chamomile. Dilute 2% of either oil in a base oil and then slowly massage into the affected part.

6. Herpes Zoster (Shingles)

Lavender oil for local use, and infusion of Lavender flowers. Avena Sativa (oat straw) tincture (20 drops). Add Rosemary's infusion to it if there is excessive depression. Take a cup of tea of lime Blossom in the evening.

Oils : Choose from Tea Tree oils, Bergamet or Eucalyptus oils (in persistent pains). Use oil of Lavender for analgesic and healing properties. To yield still better results mix oils of Lavender and Bergamot or Bergamot and Tea Tree – though all the 4 oils are equally beneficial and effective.

7. Stress

For more agitated states, choose relaxing infusions from Lime Balm, Lavender, Lemon Balm or Lime Blossom. In most acute states Valerian may be used in tablet form, as its taste is disgusting/nauseating. If exhaustion has already set in, infusion of Betony or Rosemary or Vervain may be used or all the three may be mixed together. Use Oats to enhance dietary nourishment, as they fortify nervous system.

Oils : It is better to dilute/mix essential oils to vegetable oils and used as a massage or local application with soft and tender hands. For uplifting results (effects), one can choose from clary sage, Bergamot, Rosemary or Geranium; though Merjoram or lavender are more relaxing. We cannot overlook brilliant depression relieving (Ed-stressing) properties of Jasmine, Neroli and Rose even if they are quite costly – Naroli is refreshing and anti-depressent, Rose is relaxing and calming, and Jasmine is an almost euphoric and relaxing – but all these need to be used very sparingly, sparsely and in minimal quantity.

8. Asthma

In crisis stage, seek advice of a professional but in-between the attacks prepare a mixture of infusions of Eyebright, Lavender and Chamomile so that airways get relaxed, mucus membranes are toned up, and irritability and inflammation of the bronchi get reduced.

Oils : Drop some drops of Chamomile/Lavender/Berganot/ Frankin cense on a hanky/tissue paper/piece of small cloth and sniff in aroma of any one of the referred essential oils. For local massage, use diluted oil on the chest & sideways. It will clear the chest and also prevent building up of tenacious mucus that creates a wheeze. It will also prevent spasms.

9. Colds

Take equal quantity of Yarrow, Elderflower and Peppermint and blend all the three, for being taken at the bed-time or an hour earlier. Take powder of Cayenne (Capsicum Minimum) 1.25ml or ¼ of a teaspoon and add to the above infusion. Grate fresh ginger and mix with Cinnamon powder.

Oils : Take warm water bath at night, adding 10 drops each of Lavender and Cinnamon oils. During the day-bath add 10 drops of Eucalyptus oil to water.

10. Catarrh

Catmint (Nepeta Cataria) infusion will ease nasal congestion and clear nasal congestions to facilitate breathing. Elder flower (sambucus Nigra) is anti-inflammatory, eases mucus secretion and reduces swelling of (nasal) muscus membranes. Hyssop has the properties of facilitating breathing by loosening up thick and tenacious phlegm, will induce sleep if it is disturbed due to breathing problem. Goldern Rod (Solidago Virgaurea) is an astringent, hence is capable of reducing excessive mucus and toning up the mucus membranes.

11. Bronchitis

Take infusions of Hyssop, Marshmallow, Thyme or use white Hore hound (Marribium Vulgare) to soothe harsh and painful coughs. Garlic is the most powerful anti-infective agent which will facilitate expectoration of excessive mucus and help to build up resistance in all respiratory infections.

Oils : Gently rub eucalyptus oil on the chest or use olive oil to it. Take a bowl of hot water, add 2-3 drops of lavender/ Eucalyptus/Thyme or Tea tree essential oil and inhale the medicated steam but make sure, the boiling water does not fall on your body.

12. Coughs

Remember you cannot expecorate unless there is coughing. Use following herbs as per indications. Hyssop is useful when cough is associated with irritation and restivity. It is a calming and relaxing expectorate. Coltfoot (Tusilago Farfara) will soothen and loosen cough, reduce the spasm, remove spasmodic and irritating cough. Marshmallow (Althea officinalis) is a demulcent; hence soothes the inflamed aire tubes, Thyme (Thymus Vulgaris) is a powerful antiseptic, relieves dry cough which is associated with some respiratory infection.

13. Sore Throat

Use infusions of Thyme, Sage, Agrimony which are astringents or, still better, tincture to gain quick relief. Even sucking of liquorice sticks will soothe an inflammed throat, or add liquorice sticks to above three ingredients. A drop of essential oil of lemon in ¼ TSP (2.5ml) honey, taken orally, will soothe and disinfect throat.

14. Sinusitis

To reduce infection, soothe throat membranes, and lessen infection, use oils of lavender, eucalyptus, thyme, pine, peppermint or Tea tree, either singally or in combination form, and inhale steam once or twice day. In acute cases, inhalations may be had even 4 times in a day. Eucatyptus oil, by far, is the best choice for steam inhalation. further, in order to loosen and liquefy thick mucus and remove nasal congestion catmint, golden Seal (Cannabis Candensis), though quite expensive, has cooling, toning and astringent effects – 500 mg of the drug will suffice as a daily single dose. Elder Flower is more useful in chronic state. It eases congestion and improves blood circulation. Raw garlic cloves or garlic pearls are also useful remedies as a long term measure.

15. Tonsillitis

Myrrh, Thyme and Sage are useful remedies in this. Condition, apart from other remedies mentioned for sore throat. Cone Flower (Echinacea Augustifolia) is an excellent remedy for repeated attacks of tonsillitis. Essential oils are not be used internally but may be utilised here, as a supportive device, for steam inhalations, such as thyme/Eucalyptus for infection and inflammation.

16. Influenza

Prepare tea by mixing powder of Cinnamon (500 mg or 1gm) and take such tea 3-4 times daily to induce sweating. To fortify this tea, add ginger powder. Sweating can also be induced by taking infusions of catmint and elderflower. If there is much pain in muscles and bones, take Passiflora incarnata or Boneset, either alone or in combination with above-mentioned herbs. To offset other complications use garlic paste/chopped small pieces with bread or mixed with honey.

Drop 4-5 drops each of eucalyptus and menthol oils to a bowl of hot water and inhale. It will also stop spread of infection and, if taken at the initial signs of cold, it will offset complications.

17. Fever

Specific types of fevers are not being dealt with here, rather general fever-due to heat/cold is being prescribed for to encourage sweating. Drop (1%) dilution of oils (4-5 drops) like Lavender or Tea Tree, Cypress, Chamomile into Vegetable oil (mustard, coconut) and massage over chest and back. To make it still stronger, add 5 drops of Lavender, Peppermint or Eucalyptus to the above oils and gently massage over chest, back, neck, nose, throat. Later remedies have cooling effect, hence avoid using in winter/cold winds.

Orally take tea of ginger (grated pieces of fresh root), Cinnamon powder (½TSP or 2.5 mg). If there is restivity and sweating caused by taking infusions of Elder flower or high fever still persists, then sweating can be induced by taking-infusions of Catmint, Boneset, Peppermint and Yarrow. General relaxation and blood circulation should better be brought by adding Lime Blossom. Hyssop is another remedy to quell symptoms like poor circulation and bring in general relaxation of body.

18. Acidity & Heartburn

The two conditions are caused by ingestion of heavy, rich,

spicy, diet, heavily laden with ghee/oil. It can also be triggered by eating food hastily. Those who drink and smoke heavily also suffer from acidity and heartburn, in addition to flatulence, colic and general dyspepsia. Remove the basic factors that are known causes of such disturbances. Repeated bouts of acidic dyspepsia need help of a professional.

Chamomile is relaxant, anti-inflammatory remedy that tones up digestion, provided acidity is caused by eating rich foods and stress. Lemon Balm will be also helpful, if stress is major cause of complant. Meadow sweet/Filipendula Ulmaria), though aspirin/or say salicylates also reduces acidity, provided a person is not sensitive to aspirin and other derivatives.

Slippery Elm (Ulmus Fulva) soothes the inflamed stomach or gullet and will justify its name by going down, coating and soothing the mucus membranes of digestive system. Mix a TSP in water or take tablets.

Excessive acidity can be dispelled by using hot compresses of Chamomile/Lavender (10 drops) in a bowl of water and then used. It will give almost instant relief from spasm and inflammation which generally accompany hyperacidity. If the discomfort is too great, add 1-2 drops of oils of either of these oils to base oil and then applied over whole abdomen, or more so on the area (abdominal) affected most.

Take lemon juice, (mixed with a cup of water) and add some rock salt to taste. This may be taken 1-2 hours prior to taking meals, or lemon may be used with meals. It will also remove constipation-one of the contributory causes of acidity.

19. Flatulence

Accumulation of gas in the intestines/stomach is merely an occasional/isolated symptom which occurs consequent upon taking food, in excess, that contains wind-producing foods. If it is a chronic problem, then it may indicate irritable Bowel Syndrome or Diverticulitis which require attention of a physician.

Normally the gas passes out after sometime of its accumulation, without causing much discomfort.

If stomach is the seat of problem, you can choose from Chamomile, Lemon Balm, Catmint, Peppermint. If small intestines are the seat of problem, then add Fennel or Dill to above-mentioned herbs. For bowel flatulence, add ginger. 5 drops of Essential Oils of Fennel, Caraway, Chamomile, Marjoram and Peppermint may be mixed (any one or more, depending on gravity of the malady) with hot water and applied in the form of hot compresses over painful area.

Since flatulence is common problem with those who eat too much and too often of fried and rich foods, eat rather hastily. If food is taken while one is tense, or as if one is on the run while he grabs/swallows his food. As a preventive and corrective measure, do not bend, sit curled up on a low sofa, immediately after taking meals as, by doing so, you will simply help the gas to build up, thereby causing bloating of abdomen which can have colicky pains. Simple self-management in dietary intake will suffice to enable you stay free from flatulence and colic.

20. Colic

Colic is the resultant end of a flatulent situation and the factors leading to both the situations do not vary much. Food bereft of dietary fibre, lack of proper and adequate physical activity, trapping of gas in the abdomen/intestives, constipated bowels, bouts of cramping pains colic is a common complaint of babies who ought to be treated by a professional. Repeated bouts of colic point to some chronic digestive problem and, if neglected, it may lead to even serious complications; hence never neglect the chronic stage of colic. Every abdominal pain should not always be attributed to indigestion, constipation or flatulence, rather some serious symptom may be lying latent/undetected.

Colic attacks, which are not frequent, can be controlled by taking hot teas of Chamomile, Catmint, Ginger, Fennel or

Peppermint. Use Aromatic seeds of Aniseed, Caraway, Dil, or Fennel in food or else chew the seeds after meals. Massage oil of Fennel, Peppermint or Chamomile over the abdomen in a clockwise direction, using small circles to massage the colon as well. Renal colic should not be confounded with abdominal colic as, in the latter case, pain is rhythmic and travels from loins to grain but in the former it simply revolves within the abdomen and is relieved when stools are passed or wind/gas is expelled.

21. Constipation

Constipation is considered to be the key factor for onset and progress of many body ailments, as per Ayurvedic theory which believes that if your digestion is in order, stools are passed without any hassels, wind is discharged freely/gas is eructated, your body secrets sweat regularly, you are not likely to face any (major) health hazard. Constipation is a common symptom (not a disease) of those whose diet is devoid of milk products, green and leafy vegetables, roughage, sufficient amount of vitamins and minerals. Chronic suffering may lead to incarcerated flatus, pain while passing stools, pain in rectum and anus, occasional passage of blood while passing (hard and knotty) stools, foul smell, general discomfort, abdominal pain. Increase of the' missing ingredient in diet, as stated above, will prevent occurrence of constipation. Belching after meals is said to be a welcome sign of quick digestion of food. In addition, Yogic exercises, physical exercises, walking, inhaling plenty of fresh and pure air, leading an active and busy life help to digest food, thus ruling out any possibility of constipation.

It may be noted that constipation is the probable cause behind onset of colic, flatulence, acidity, gas formation, acidity. If your bowels are regular, you are not likely to suffer from anyone of the disorder. For recent constipation take a TSP of Isabghole husk with a glass of hot milk at night, before retiring to bed. It will also improve general health condition.

Another useful remedy is Triphala (a combination of Harar, Bahera and Amla) which should be taken at bed time with a glass of lukewarm water or hot milk. Either of the said medicines will remove both acute and chronic constipation which is generally of three types, as detailed below.

(i) Either the stools are not passed even once daily or for many days or

(ii) One has to frequently visit the closet to pass stools but the quantity passed, each time, is quite small and there is always a feeling that 'something remained' in the intestines.

(iii) When perstaltic action of intestines and rectum is sluggish and weak. In this situation either the so intestine is unable to push the faecal matter to rectum or rectum itself is unable to push out or expel stools due to weak or lost peristalsis.

In any case, avoid taking laxatives or purgatives to ease constipation-once the habit of taking such pills build up, it becomes a habit, and stools will not be passed without intake of such pills which are habit forming.

Take decoction of Dandalion root and liquorice sticks. If this formula fails, take 2TSP or 10ml of linseed with water (250-300ml) at breakfast. Better coarse would be to soak the said quantity of linseed in water at night. It will absorb liquid and create a soft bulk so as to promote peristaltic wave movements. But don't forget to take plenty of water orally.

Add 2 drops of Rosemary, lavender or Marjoram to base oil and massage gently on the abdomen clockwise, in addition to taking anyone of the remedies detailed above.

22. Chilblains

This a condition of red, round itching of the skin, occuring generally in winter/cold weather on the fingers and toes. The underlying cause being poor circulation of blood and depleted supply of oxygen to the fingers and toes. When cells of skin are damaged, redness and swelling, itching occur, due to impact of cold conditions. Use of radiant heat, like warming by fire can also cause burning, itchy sensation and swelling. In certain situations even bleeding may also take place.

Main purpose is to improve circulation in the extremities, for which use hand and foot bath, by adding decoction of fresh ginger roots to (warm) water in the proportion of ½ oz (15gm) of ginger decoction to 3/4 litre of water or, for optimum circulation, use also caynne (capsicum minimum) — the latter should not be used when the skin is broken. Take teas prepared out of the said ingredients. In addition, use also infusion of yarrow that will dilate small blood vessels in the hands and feet.

For local applications (provided the skin is not broken) massage with essential oils of Ginger, Marjoram or Black pepper (3% quantity) to any vegetable oil – This being a short term measure. For long term measure, use oils of Juniper, pines, Rosemary or cypress, as directed above, and dilute them in a base (oil) only, for being massaged briskly over hands and feet. Ginger tea may be used internally also.

23. Piles

Piles are either dry or bleeding and often caused by chronic constipation, hard and knotty sloots, intake of spices, wines, meats and also by poor or absent physical activity. Dry piles is more painful, while bleeding piles render a person weaker. Pregnant ladies, elderly persons, sedentary persons who eat enormously and quite often but do no exercise, or the person taking above-mentioned dietary items, are more prone to piles. Persistant complaint may cause other complications also, such as fissures, cancerous growths, pain, swelling, smarting etc. Use the remedies suggested under constipation.

Use oil of Cypress/Juniper in the bath or using some drops of either to a bowl of cold water for improving circulation. Abdomen should be massaged with a 2% oil dilution, to any vegetable oil (used as a base oil) of Rosemary or Marjoram.

Apply locally commercial creams processed from the extracts of morse chestmt (Aescutus hippocastanum), Pilecort

.(Ranunculus ficaria) or Marigold (Calendula officinalis). Tincture of distilled witch Hazel (Hamamelis Virginiana) is astringent and can be safely used as a compress. It will also provide relief in prolonged bleeding which can also be prevented by using tea prepared from Nettle (Urtica Deocca).

All the ointments/creams, mentioned above, are available from homeopath pharmacists/retailers. Remember, frequent and profuse bleeding is liable to cause general weakness and anaemia also, hence don't let it prolong. I feel use of caster oil with milk (1TSP with a warm cup of tea, or, still better, Isabghole Husk (1TSP) with warm milk will help in softening stool and, thus, cause easy and (almost) painless passage thereof. Third alternative being to take a TSP of Triphala with water at bed-time. You can choose any of the said ingredients, as per individual suitability and convenience, but I would opt for Isabghule for obvious reasons.

24. Retarded/Poor Blood Circulation

Though seemingly it is does not appear to be a symptom of much consequence/effect, it can lead to disorders like thromobosis or Phlebitis which are quite serious manifestations. Poor circulation is not uncommon in cold climates, advanced age, pregnancy, sedentary way of life. Paramount need is to nip the problem at the inception stage. It is necessary to know and pin point the basic contributory factors that lead to this situation. The onset is gradual and the patient comes to know of it only when the malady has assumed serious portents.

Dilute oils of Rosemary, Black pepper, Marjoram or Lavender (10 drops) or else 2-3 oils can be mixed to base oil. Massage into hands and feet with a steady circular movement. Fingers, soles, palms should be gently massaged.

Garlic is an excellent remedy to push up and improve blood circulation. In addition to ginger, cynine Pepper is, by far, the strongest one to stimulate circulation, and both can be used as regular part of daily diet. Herbal teas, prepared from Ginger, Yarrow, Nettle, Lime Blossom or Elder flower, are equally useful to improve circulation. If numbness persists, despite adherance to the said devices, it is better to seek help of a professional lest the disease gets out of control.

25. Vericose Veins

The condition implies swollen veins, particularly in the legs, but may occur elsewhere also. Veins in the legs contain one-way valves which allow blood to flow back up towards the heart. If, for instance, muscles of calves weaken (due to poor nutrition, obesity, pregnancy, lack of physical activity, in old age, after prolonged standing) the valves fail to function efficiently as a consequence of which the blood stagnates and collects in the veins, causing swelling. The veins look like a bunch of tangled ropes, and their prominence is quite visible.

As a supportive measure, do not let the legs hand down, rather keep them slightly raised above the thigh-level, by keeping a cushion or pillow under the feet, making an angle of 60°, so that gravity helps the venous system. Prepare diluted version of essential oils (dilution) by mixing base (vegetable) oil to (essential) oils of chamomile, cypress or even Juniper, and massage the vericosed veins and areas around, in the upward direction (going from downwards towards the heart side) to reduce congestion.

Prepare a dilution of water and tinctures (50:50) of Witch Hazel, Marigold and apply externally over the vericosed area. Lime Blossom infusion is capable of improving peripheral blood circulation, whereas Horse chestnut (Aesculus Hippocastanum) may be taken (30 drops twice daily) in water, or else its tablets.

Herbal treatment can be more effective if regular and sustainable physical activity is also resorted to, as both are complementary to each other.

26. Premenstrual Problems (PMS)

This is also called 'Premenstrual Syndrome' which is attributed to hormonal imbalance, due to depraved hormonal production. There is great change in attitude, temperament, behaviour, mood, approach to life (due to physical changes and mental agitation, social problems, mental approach and surroundings) This is a trying period for the growing young girls whose sex maturation is on the anvil I would like to caution adolescent girls that PMS as a natural course and they must not get upset over changes in the body organs, voice, attitude and mood. It is simply a passing phase and most of the problems, if at all they are termed as problems, get resolved by onset of menses. Sincere, timely and friendly guidance, reassurance and genuine sympathy can help the young girl to successfully overcome most, if not all, of the problems.

General and often felt symptoms include, irritability, mood changes, headache or even migraine, weepiness, tender breasts, fluid retention.

Berries of chaste tree help to normal restoration of hormonal functioning — by raising up progestrone levels because progestrone factor is the key factor. The berries should be used in tablet form. If ever some irritation is felt under the skin, at once stop its use. Herbs like Couch Grass (Agropyron Repens) or Cleavers (Galium Aparine) have diuretic properties – take infusions to seek relief. Chamomile is a gentle relaxant and diuretic, while Lemon Balm (Melessa offinalis) eases emotive feelings that tend to upset mind and cause emotional swings.

Another useful herb, introduced into the realm of herbs, is Evening Primrose (aenothera biennis) which is extolled for balancing the hormonal swings. Take 1-2 gms capsules of this herb daily – in the II half of menstrual cycle.

Essential oils of Rosemary, Juniper, Grapefriut or Geranium can be used in bath and skin can also be massaged/brushed with it.

27. Menstrual Problems

These problems can be classifed as under :

(i) **Amenorrhoea :** The state points to lack of periods which can be caused by mental trauma, emotional upsets, physical debility, loss of weight, anorexia (loss of or absence of appetite), poor health and low haemoglobin (Hb) in blood, poor diet. The situation may occur due to pregnancy, menopause, some organic problem etc.

(ii) **Dysmenorrhoea :** It means painful mensturation which can be caused by sedentary life, too much sexual indulgence, weak health, inadequate or/and spicy diet, anaemia, general run-down condition of health, strain and stress of circumstantial origin.

(iii) **Menorrhagia :** It means excessive bleeding during menstruation. Common causes are abortion, accident, miscarriage, rape, tumor, forceful coition. It may result in acute anaemia. Every bleeding from the passage should not be taken as menstrual bleeding.

Herbs can play an effective role in meeting most of the menstrual problems as they have curative and corrective effects on hormones and their approache is holistic. Take infusion of Chamomile or Lemon Balm, to have relief in painful periods. A decoction of Cramp Bark or Valerian is a useful way to get rid of severe Cramping pains. Since their taste is disgusting, so better take in tablet form (maximum dose : 5gm in divided doses).

28. Menopause/Menopausal Syndrome

The term simply means cessation of mesntrual process. As puberty is a trying time for the young girls, so is menopause for the elderly ladies. Though there are no hard and fast rules as to the cessation of menses, it is held that a woman ceases to menstruate between 45-50 years. Truly speaking, every woman is a law unto herself and no yardstick can be applied to onset and end of menses, but a woman is generally known to menstruate for 30-35 years. This is a critical time for the ladies, though all do not suffer the similar consequences. As mentioned earlier, every cessation of bleeding must not be taken as an end to menses, as it can happen in-between periods, during anaemic conditions, pregnancies and organic defects.

For some of the ladies it is a period of relief while for others, there could be anxiety, flushes, insomnia, heavy bleeding, depression, severe vaginal dryness, feeling of 'out of sorts', disinclination to work, slothness, mental agitation etc which are sufficient to make her life misearable. But, as soon as menses cease, all the said and other problems disappear. Disproportinate and profuse bleeding must be treated, alongwith other disturbing symptoms.

Sage is an excellent herb to dispel problems like depression, hot sweats, irritability. It has oestrogenic effects and activity which eases drop in hormonal levels which tend to upset the entire system. Two infusions in a days would generally suffice, but has to be continued for about 3 or 4 weeks. But barries of chaste tree are said to ·have more salutary effects, as it acts through the pituitary gland, thus encouraging the ovaries. It can be taken in tablet form (300mg per day) or in tea form. Since it can cause itching in the skin, it should not be taken in an overdose.

Lime Blossom or Chamomile are good relaxants and can reduce emotional fluctuations quite well. Seek a specialist's advice if symptoms do not yield to such herbs.

Use Rose and/or Geranium oil for general uplift and oils of Jasmine, Neroli or Bergamot for dealing with emotional swings. These oils can be used during bath, by dropping a few drops in water or used as massage over the skin by adding a few drops in the base oil (1% solution), but only one kind of oil must not be used continuously, rather alternate with other oils.

29. Morning Sickness

Most of the pregnant women experience nausea and vomiting during pregnancy – but more particularly in the first trimester. It is a natural consequence and does not warrant any medicine or expert's advice but, if the symptoms are persistantly severe, medical help must not be delayed. The sickness can occur at any time during a period of 24 hours, but is most common during the day. It is generally caused by low sugar content in the blood which state can be averted if the lady takes food at regular intervals. Nausea can prevent taking of food; hence it must be treated but violent vomiting must be treated, as it can lead to miscarriage/abortion.

Ginger is a herb of choice but no oils should be used. Chew a piece of ginger with some rock salt, if taste permits or sip tea made from freshly peeled ginger. Tea should be sipped frequently. Best method is to eat ginger biscuits, one of which can be nibbled as an when necessary. It will push up sugar level in the body and also give curative effect of ginger. Teas of Peppermint and Chamomile are also equally beneficial but, if smell of Chamomile or any other herbs is disagreeable, then it never be persisted with, rather it should be substituted by another one.

30. Thrush

It is a common name for a fungal infection of mucus membranes caused by the yeast Candida Albicans which can affect mouth, (even of tiny babies), on the penis or around the anus but it is a vaginal infection that is triggered by (excessive) use of antibiotics that destroy defensive bacteria which help to fight the infection(s). This infection can recur, hence if cured once, should not be taken as a sign of permanent cure.

Inflammation of bladder (cystitis), high sugar diet, contraceptive pills, general emotional upsets and run-down conditions can also trigger thrush. Oil of Tea Tree is a natural anti-fungal and soothing agent. use 6 drops of oil in water, and wash the vaginal area. Oils of Myrrh and lavender could be used, either blending either or both with Tea Tree oil to hasten the healing process.

Cone Flower (Echinancea angustifolia) and Marigold (calendula officinalis) have also anti-fungal properties. Dilute 1TSP to 600ml of water (either of the two herbs) and use as a local wash. It can also be applied to baby's mouth, by soaking a cotton swab in it. In case of adults, put a TSP in little water and use in the form of a mouth-wash. For recurring thrush, garlic is an excellent remedy which may be used locally, but can irritate inflamed vaginal membranes. In order to obviate the problem of irritation, peel a garlic clove and dip in olive oil and insert in the vagina where it should be left overnight. But, do not forget to tie a thread to it (so that it is not left in the Vagina) and remove the same in the next morning. Be guarded in respect of sensitivity to Garlic.

31. Arthritis

In common parlance inflammation of joints is known as Arthritis. Though there over 80 types of arthritis, yet Osterasthritis (OA) and Rheumatoid (RA) are the two principle sub-divisions. The former is a condition that denotes natural wear and tear of joints which often follows ageing. Persons who have suffered injuries previously, either through accidents or sports (known as sports Injuries also) farming occupation, artists who have to squat due to job compulsions, domestic servants, housewives. OA rarely occurs in young age but is quite common as the age advances. Here, wear and tear of joints is a natural consequence. Ultimately the cartilege weakens and gaps between bones get reduced, resulting in cricking voice on movement or bending the joint. Knees have to mainly bear the brunt of O.A.

R.A. is an auto-immune disorder where synovial memberanes that line the joints, get inflamed and thickened, leading to pain and deformity of joints. If either of the disorders restricts or impedes physical movement or immobility of the affected joints, the problem becomes compounded.

Main aim should be to detoxify the body, improve circulation and mobility of joints, at least to the extent that patient is enabled to discharge his normal functions or, at least, does not have to lead an infirm and inactive person's life. The patients are warned not to take recourse to surgical methods, or if that be necessary, it should be the last option, when all other methods have proved futile and ineffective. General principle is to touch the affected joint (for surgical operations) only when total mobility is lost.

There is pain, swelling, heat and redness on and around the joints and patient's mobility and normal activity is adversely affected. Here the curative methods are described in relation to O.A only. There are plenty of herbs which have proven Curative faculties.

To remove acidic toxins, crush celery seeds and take as tea (5ml or 1TSP) which has an alkaline effect. To make the above prepared tea much stronger, add Parsley (5ml/1TSP0 to it. To make the tea still stronger, add a chopped small piece of ginger to it. Meadowsweat and Feverfew have better anti-inflammatory properties – Feverfew should be taken in tablet form. Even one can chew 3 fresh leaves of feverfew, but it may cause ulcers in the mouth, hence it is better to use it in tea.

Circulation around the joints can be improved through tissue-cleaning properties of essential oils of Juniper, Cypress and Lemon, whereas oils of Lavender, Rosemary and chamomile have mild analgesic and high anti-inflammatory properties. These oils can be massaged, used by diluting in water before taking bath, or else massaged/used as a compress over the affected parts. It is better to use one or two oils at a time or alternate any other two oils, but overuse must be avoided. Rosemary, Marjoram, Ginger, Pepper can be used with advantage to stimulate circulation.

Take 1-2 capsules of cod liver oil daily, use hot/cold water, according to local weather conditions. Food should include plenty of fresh vegetables. Eliminate high carbohydrate-protein and meat diet. Epsom salts (4 TBSP) should be added to bathing water, to reduce inflammation and stiffness of joints. The methods, mentioned in this para, pertain to naturopathy but can be tried to gain better and quicker results.

32. Rheumatism

This is a general term applied to inflammatory processes

in the joints or muscles, but here only muscular rheumatism will be dealt with. Sometimes, even 'fibrositis' is also placed under Rheumatism (Please read the next caption for relevent details); hence, whenever dealing with either of the disorders, refer to the other disorder and also the suggested line of treatment.

Dandalion is the remedy of choice – its leaf has diuretic quality, that increases output from the kidneys, while its root is a mild laxative and liver tonic. Make infusion of its leaves and decoction from its root, and use both for about 7-days. While Nettel is a great cleanser of blood and also rich in minerals, it helps also the repair and renewal of tissues. Both remedies can be combined to yield optimum favourable results. To relieve extreme pain Meadowsweat is recommended. Nettle and Meadowsweat infusions can be used for the purpose.

Ginger is known for its pushing up circulatory property, and can be added to either of the above said infusions. Ginger plays a significant role in Arthritis and Rheumatism.

For local treatment, essentials oil are required to cleanse the tissue and drain out toxities. For this purpose oils of Juniper, Pin, Cypress and Rosemary are required, whereas lavender oil will and aid in greater muscular relaxation, if added to anyone of the said list of oils. Stiffness and pain can be got rid of by blending Rosemary and lavender oils or Marjoram and Juniper may be added (2% of oils to vegetable base oils). It will improve blood supply to muscles and also help in speedy removal of toxins. Massage with oil is an ideal method which can resotre near-normal movements, remove stiffness and swelling from the joints. Once waste material has been removed, most (if nor all) the symptoms will disappear or, at least, show considerable improvement.

33. Gout

If kidneys fail to excrete excessively produced uric acid, the acid crystallizes into sharp tiny deposits (like small needles) and collects and deposits on and around small joints. Gout affects small joints while large joints are affected in arthritis. Such deposits collect around toes/feet, fingers of hands. Rise of uric acid is a pointer to excessive use of proteins. Hence gouty persons should avoid fish, soya, meats, vegetable oils, milk and its products.

Since there is enormous inflammation, the affected parts should be subjected to cold or cool compresses only, to tone down discomfort, for which fennel, Juniper, lemon, cypress or Pine oil should be used – either in the bathing water or compress. As soon as the inflammations subside, use Rosemary/Lavendar oils to induce warmth and flush out toxins from the joints.

Take Celery seeds in the form of tea (5ml seeds-fully crushed). Boil the seeds in 300ml water and take 3 such doses in a day. It will excrete uric acid. If necessary Meadowsweat, Devil's claw or willow Bark may also be added to celery seeds, as these three herbs are more anti-inflammatory. Nettle is a general cleansing herb which should be drunk twice a day (dose: one cup).

34. Acne (Pimples on Face)

It is the most disturbing problem at puberty when the young persons of both sexes, see pimples appearing on their face. If plucked/broken, blood/pus ooz out from pimply eruptions which leave back black scars on the face. Skin's sebaceous glands get activated due to hormonal activity. If skin is too much oily more lubricant is released due to hyperactivity of glands, which, in turn, infects and blocks hair follicles. The young persons are advised not to break/squeeze the erupted spots, otherwise the infection will spread to the surrounding areas (of tissues). If acne persists even beyond puberty, professional help will be needed. Persons with oily skin are more likely to suffer from severe infection.

Lemon, Lavender, Bergamot, Geramium are most effective herbs which should be used according to skin condition. Any one of the oils, depending on skin sensitivity of a person, should be used in some vegetable base oil. You can choose from coconut oil or grapeseed oils as base oils, If irritation persists or if there is some other reaction, at once stop further use of the oil. Only 1-2% essential oil should be used in a carrier oil.

Infusion of herbs, such as Hazel, Marigold, Elder flower, Lavender will cleanse the skin and astringency. Bedrock is a great tissue cleanser, encourages removal of waste matter from the skin through the blood supply. Use its root in the decoction and leaves for infusion. Take 3 TBSP thrice a day, which will first stir up the skin, and then improve the condition.

Red clover, Cone Flower or Dandalion may be used to aid resistance, immune stimulancy. If these herbs are used together, it will have multiple benefits but total quantity used must not exceed 3 TBSP a day. Infusion of Red clover can also be applied locally over and then washed with water.

An advice to the elders – they should not pass uncharitable and disturbing remarks or pass even negative comments to let the young adolescents feel inferior or slighted. Do not ever criticise them nor run them down. Nine out of ten adolescents pass through acne problem and there is nothing unusual in it. It should be taken in normal stride. In all cases, high standards of personal hygienic, balanced diet, congenial environs, gay and happy mood will go a long way in paving the way for quicker recovery. use of alcohol, tobacco, drugs, strong spieces must be ensured. Keep the bowels clean, inhale natural fresh air and take to long walks, participate in games, keep away from tension and worries. If you can do this much, you will help yourself to quicker recovery, even with minimum medication.

35. Boils

An acute infected and inflamed area on the skin is called a 'boil' – in a blocked hair follicle. Boils appear together, may have several pus-filled heads with large inflamed lump (called 'Furuncle' or 'Carbuncle'). Frequent recurrence of boils points to furunculosis.

Keep the boil clean and free from bacterial infection by washing the area 3-4 times a day, with the help of 2% dilution of lavender oil (essential oil), using sterile cotton wool (preferably) or a clean piece of cloth (cotton). To draw pus out of the boil, it is necessary to apply Tea Tree, Bergamot, lavender or chamomile oils which have the qualities of speedy healing, antiseptic properties, and are anti-inflammatory also. They can be used (any one of the oils) in bathing water for general detoxifying effects. Lavender oil is a remedy of choice for local application (in diluted form), gentle massage, used during bath. Marshmallow/Slippery Elm (Ulmus Fulva) poultice is quite beneficial. The latter is rightly called a herbalist's Knife due to its ability to burst the boils. You can use its paste over boils to get desired effects or else powdered root of Marshmallow or leaves can be used. After the boil has burst, clean the area and then apply cooked lavender or poultice of Slippery Elm to induce quick healing. Garlic may be rubbed over the area, after cutting the clove.

If boils frequently reappear and do not yield to home remedies, seek help of a professional. Do not pluck/break the boils to avoid spread of infection to surrounding areas.

36. Eczema

It is an allergic, inflammatory and irritating skin infection. It can be caused by wrist watches and strap, (of metal), zinc coated jeans, straps, perfumes and scents, hairdyes, fur, hair of (pet) animals, certain colours, synthetic clothes, dust, mould spores, certain plants, flowers, vegetables, bright sunlight or extremely cold winds. Holistic approach is called for to look for other allergens and disease-related causes. Some allergens and hypersensitivity thereto is quite well known to many patients who, by avoiding the same, can stay free from eczema. Certain insecticides, pesticides, fumes, gases can also be trigger points. The problem needs to be looked into minutely ascertain causes of allergy, so as to caution the patient accordingly.

Oils of Lemon Balm, Geranium, Chamomile or lavender can be used in 1% or still lower concentration by mixing with acqeous cream, thicker cream, vegetable oil or ointment. It is prudent to watch reaction on the skin of all these herbal oils, by testing them on your skin one-by-one. Oil compresses are useful when the involved area is large. Drop 5 drops to ½ litre water and then use.

To hasten healing and reduce inflammation, use Marigold or Comfrey. Prepare a cream or ointment from either of the said herbal oils and apply locally. Chickweed (stellaria Media) is of unquestioned value to calm itching which is a common feature of eczema. You can use it in the form or cream/ointment, or prepare an infusion and then use as a cold compress, which will suit more when the eczema is dry. For moist or weeping eczema, apply, in neat or cream form, Red clover or Hearteas. Oil (diluted in some vegetable oil) of Evening Primrose will give soothing and healing relief, if applied locally.

Nettle and Red clover possess quality of blood-cleaning, and should be used in the form of infusions. Decoctions of yellow Dock or Burdock can also be used for the said purpose. Dandalion root is extolled as toner of liver. It also gently clears the bowels but should be used as a decoction. Cleavers (Galium Aparme) is also famous for removing toxins through kidneys, but should be used as an infusion. You can mix up both the herbs and prepare a mixture but must not be used beyond three weeks.

37. Spots on Face

Appearance of any type of spot on face is not taken kindly by any person, as spots and blamishes give ugly look to the face which disturb the young persons, both boys and girls, ladies and elders alike. When pimples are plucked, facial skin is bound to have blemishes/spots which are a common sight at puberty.

For instant disappearance of spots, rub raw garlic over the affected portion. In certain persons it may irritate the skin, hence abandon its use as soon as some reaction is noticed.

Prepare a paste from leaves of fresh comfrey (a handful), one clove of garlic fully mashed and honey. Paste, so processed, should be applied over a warmed leaf of cabbage and then applied over the affected area before going to bed. Let the application remain on the face for an hour or so, after which it should be washed off with lukewarm water, patting the face gently with a towel.

Take 2 TBSP of crystal clear and pure honey and mix 1 TSP of sunflower oil and 1TSP of wheat germ – mix all the three ingredients to make a thick paste which should be applied over face and neck (but protect your eyes in all facial & local applications. Let the applied paste stay for 5 minutes, whereafter wash it off with warm water. Pat dry the face and neck with a towel or with your hands. Avoid using soap or any other facial cream/lotion in-between.

Both the above mentioned prescriptions are considered quite safe and effective but reactions to certain individuals cannot be ruled out or denied.

38.   Nettle Rash/Urticaria/Hives

The disease is caused by taking some disagreeable food item, exposure to cold weather, heat of sun, reaction to chemicals, gases, fumes, dust, polens. The causatives are many and it takes hell of time and labour to work out and discern the real culprit (allergen). Some persons are hypersensative to colours, animals, animal skins, spices and condiments. In short, anything under the sun can cause allergic reactions and Nettle Rash is one of such reactions. The patient is restless, has eruptions all over the body, profusely scratches his body but every time he itches, the subsequent result is far worse. Generally, there is no fever but constipation and interrupted urine may be there. When the eruptions manifest in the eyes and throat, the patient's condition worsens. Unless the cause is found out, the malady will continue to torment the patient, at any time any place. There are wheals and blisters on the skin in majority of cases, but some may be having only rashes or eruptions, though stinging sensation and itching are almost common to all the patients.

Irritation can be mollified and calmed down by applying

calamine lotion which has soothing and cooling effect. Some experts maintain that nettle tea should be given. Stinging sensation and discomfort can be controlled by rubbing leaves of dock.

Before concluding this chapter, it is necessary to point out that only very common diseases have been taken up which normally cause immense sufferings to people. The suggestions given, with regard to use of certain herbs, should be taken merely as an indicative guidance. Normally a patient is not expected to treat himself for all his illnesses, but the common and general ailments can be easily managed at home, provided there is no reaction, though more complex and serious ailments should be better left to the physician for treatment. Many factors could cause an ailment, hence each cause has to be ascertained before any remedy is decided for administration. Readers are advised to go through the description and therapeutic, efficacy of various herbs and their ability to cure various disorders, as given in sufficient detail in the pages that follow.

Leading Healing Properties of Some Herbs

(Explained in a Nutshell)

1. Boneset (Eupatorium Poerfoliation) [Aerial Parts Used]

Promotes sweating, is antispasmodic, bitter, febrifuge, immune stimulant, laxative. use internally for Flu, common cold, fever related childs, chicken pox, measles, severe pain in bones, sluggish digestion, liver stagnation. *Its high dose might cause Vomiting.*

2. Burdock (Arctium Lappa) [Root, seeds used]

It is anti-viral, anti-allergic, anti-inflammatory; adrenal tonic, laxative, expectorant, soothes gastric muscosa, reduces levels fo blood cholesterol, has tonic effect. Used internally for asthma, coughs in chest, bronchitis, arthritis, inflammation of gastric origin, gastric ulcers, helps in recovery after use of steroids. *Do not use in high blood pressure, cirrhosis of liver, pregnancy or while taking digoxin or diagoxin based drugs or in excessive doses and prolonged use.*

3. Celery (Apium graveolans) [used in essential oils. Seeds used for medicinal purposes]

It is diuretic, carminative, anti-rheumatic, urinary antiseptic and increases excretion of uric acid. Should be used internally for disorders like gout, rheumatism, arthritis, urinary disorders, Cystitis, high blood pressure; also to increase milk flow in nursing women.

Avoid using in pregnancy. Never take seeds for cultivation internally; nor use its essential oil in skin disorders as it can increase skin photosensitivity.

4. Skull Cap (Scutellaria lateriflora) [Aerial Parts used]

It is a sedative of high order, relaxes nerves (is a Nervine tonic), digestive, cooling, stimulant, antispasmodic, anti-bacterial, lowers blood cholestorol levels. It is often used internally with advantage in disorders like excitability, stress, anxiety, Nervous exhaustion, migraine, premenstrual tension, sleeplessness (insomnia), helps to get rid of addictive tranquilisers (at withdrawal stage). It is quite frequently combined with valerian/ hops, in insomnia and sedative mixtures.

5. Dandelion (Taraxacum officinale) [Its root, leaves and sap are used]

Its roots is laxative and bile stimulant, urinary antiseptic, diuretic, antiseptic (in general), a (bitter) digestive tonic used internally for liver congestion rheumatic and skin disorders, poor appetite, indigestion, digestive weakness, reduces blood cholesterol levels. Its fresh sap is used externally for warts. It

89

is used to improvise blood flow to the heart, added to heart remedies due to rich content of potassium, and used for fluid retention in branded (patent) products.

6. Elecampane (Inula Belenium) [Flowers and roots used]

It serves as a tonic, is stimulant, expectorant, antispasmodic, anti-catarrhal, antiseptic, promotes sweating. Internally used for flu, hay fever, asthma, bronchitis, disturbing and stubborn coughs, other respiratory disorders. It is externally used in skin rashes, vericose ulcers. It is used often as an effective tonic after an attack of flu, long standing respiratory problems, and is an almost indispensable ingredient in many brands of cough syrups. Its infusion should be used as a wash for ulcers.

7. Echinacea (E.Pallida, E.Purpurea, Echinacea angustifolia) [used its root and aerial parts]

It is anti-inflammatory, anti-allergenic, anti-microbial, immune stimulant, lymphatic tonic. it heals wounds and raises W.B.C. count in the blood. Its chief internal uses include disorders like kidney infections, Flu, colds, sore throat, food poisoning, boils, acne, glandular fever. Externally its ointments and creams are used for wounds, skin infections, (infected) insect bites. *If used in high doses, dizziness and nausea can ensue, hence take proper caution.*

8. Hops (Humulus Lupulus) [Its strobules, from Female Plant, are used]

It is sedative, nerve tonic, diuretic, mild sedative, an aphrodisiac, astringent, antiseptic, antispasmodic and bitter. It is internally used in anxiety, nervous tension, insomnia, premature ejaculation, loss of appetite (Anorexia), emotional upsets during menopause. Use its infusion as a wash to slow-healing wounds, and ulcers. *Its growing plants might cause contact dermatitis. Do not use when there is depression.*

9. Hyssop (Hyssopus Officinalis) [Aerial parts and essential oils]

It is carminative, diuretic, sedative, anti-viral, anti-catarrhal, anti-viral, anti-spasmodic, expectorant, promotes sweating. It should be used internally for complaints like Flu, colds, sore throats, nervous stomach, digestive upsets, coughs, bronchitis and anxiety. Use externally for bruises and eczema (in the form of infusion as a wash); as an oil in baths and rubs in melancholy, Nervous exhaustion, cough, bronchitis. *Beware, excessive use of its essential oil can cause convulsions.*

10. Eucalyptus (Eucalyptus globulus) [leaves and essential oil used]

It is anti-viral, expectorant, anti-microbial, anti-spasmodic, expels worms and reduces sugar level in the blood. It should be used externally for lung infections, coughs, bronchitis, trapped phlegm, muscular and joint pains as an oil. Use its infusion as a gargle in sore throats; as an inhalation in bronchial and nasal congestions, infusion as a wash in wounds. Add 2-8 drops to gargles and inhalations, and essential oil should be diluted for oil massage.

11. Garlic (Allium Sativum) [Its oil and cloves are used for various therapeutic effects].

It is a high quality expectorant, bile stimulant, anti-microbial, immune stimulant, anti-microbial, reduces blood sugar and cholesterol levels in the blood. Internally it is used in infections, catarrh, as a heart and circulatory tonic, digestive disorders, and used externally for corns, warts, acne, fungal infections (as fresh cloves). Caution should be taken while using its high doses in pregnancy and breastfeeding. It can irritate sensitive stomach. Avoid heavily deodorized products. use with utmost care and caution locally for skin infections, as it may irritate and redden the senstive skin.

12. Lemon Balm (Mellisa officinalis) [used its aerial parts and essential oil].

It is carminative, digestive, stimulant, sedative, anti-depressant, anti-bacterial, anti-spasmodic, anti-viral. Used internally in nervous exhaustion, melancholy, stress, fevers, chills, indigestion. Externally it should be used as a compress in swelling, and its cream applied in case of insect bites, to repel insects. Its essential oil is used in chest congestions, anxiety, depression. It is often used in products for insomnia and anxiety and also used quite often with valerian.

13. Wild Lettuce (Lactuca Virosa) [dried juice (latex), and leaves].

It is a relaxing nervine tonic, sedative, mild analgesic, wild hypnotic, anti-spasmodic, an aphrodisiac. It is used internally for anxiety, nervous excitability, insomnia, children's hyperacidity, Nervous, persistent and irritating cough. It is often combined with passion flower and hops in insomnia. its latex was sold as a substitute for opium. *Its excessive use might cause restivity.*

14. White Dead Nettle (Lamium Album) [Its flowering tops are used].

It is anti-catarrhal, anti-spasmodic, anti-inflammatory, expectorant, diuretic, is a regulator of menses, astringent. It is used internally in heavy, irregular menstrual periods; prostate problems, cystitis, and irritable bowel syndrome. use it externally (infusion as a wash) in minor cuts and grazes (abrasions), piles. Use its infusion as an eye-bath in conjunctivities. Its tea can help a lot, if used after surgery for benign prostatic enlargement, to speed up uprecovery.

15. Rasberry (Rubas Idoeus) [used its fruit & leaves].

Used as a preparative for child birth, is an astringent, anti-spasmodic, tonic, digestive stimulant. It is used internally to ease childbirth, period (menstrual) pain and heavy menstrual bleeding and in mild diarrhoea. Externally, use its infusion as a wash in vericose ulcers, sores and wounds; leaf-infusion as a gargle/ mouth-wash in gum disease, sore throat, infusion as an eye-wash in sore eyes. *Use very cautiously in pregnancy, especially until last two months of pregnancy.*

16. Peppermint (Menthaxpeperita) [Used aerial parts and essential oil].

It is a digestive tonic, carminative, anti-spasmodic, mild sedative, prevents vomiting, promotes sweating and relaxes peripheral blood vessels.It should be used internally for digestive upsets, poor appetite, indigestion, problems of gall-bladder, nausea, colitis, nausea and vomiting. Use externally its infusion as a wash in fungal infections & skin irritations. Its oil may be used in bronchial congestion and cattarrh. *Do not serve it to breast-feeding babies. Use carefully in skin infections, as it is mucus membranes' irritant.*

17. Elder (Sambucus Nigra) [Its leaves, flowers, berries and bark used]

It is diuretic, laxative, expectorant, anti-catarrhal, stimulant, circulatory, topical anti-inflammatory (flowers). Use its flowers as a prophylactic for sore throats, mouth ulcers, hay fevers. Externally, its leaves should be used for wounds, and flowers for eye-inflammations, sores, chilblains and chapped skin. *Its bark must not be used in pregnancy, as it is a purgative.*

18. Yellow Dock (Rumex crispus) [Root is used]

It is a bile-stimulant, anti-sposmadic, anti-septic and an astringent. Internally, it should be used in various disorders of liver, especially congestion of liver, boils and irritating skin eruptions, rheumatic problems. use it externally for mouth ulcers as a mouth wash. It is abundantly used in laxative mixtures and in preparations, and used for eczema and skin rashes.

19. Valerian (Valerian officinalis) [Root used]

It reduces blood pressure, allays pain, is carminature and tranquiliser. it is used internally for high blood pressure, palpitation, anxiety, insomnia, tension headache, migraine, bronchial spasm and pains during/before menstruation. Externally, use its compress in muscular cramps; infusion as wash in ulcers and wounds. *Patients are warned not to use it with other sleep-inducing drugs, in palpitations and headache on prolonged basis.*

20. Ginger (Zingiber officinalis) [Root, essential oil]

It is carminative, expectorant, induces sweating, prevents vomiting, is anti-spasmodic, anti-septic, anti-inflammatory. It should be used internally for poor circulation, Flu, nausea, morning sickness, poor appetite, indigestion, colic, irritable bowel syndrome, menstrual cramps. Externally, use its hot infused oil in rheumatic pains. At some chemists shops, it is also available in capsules and tablets for travel sickness. Also available as ginger beer/sweets. In most of Ayurvedic preparations it is used for various therapeutic effects.

21. Heartsease (Viola Tricolor) [Aerial parts only used]

It is expectorant, diuretic, laxative, stabilizer of capillary membranes, anti-rheumatic, anti-inflammatory. It is used internally in whooping cough, bronchitis, acne, eczema. It prevents capillary bleeing. Use its cream or ointment or infusion as a wash for insect bites, skin rashes, cradle cap in babies, weeping sores. *It must not be used in high doses since it is rich in saponins (having a quality akin to soap or soaps' foam).*

22. Liquorice (Glycyrrhiza glabra) [Its root and Juice is used)

It is a tonic, soothes gastric mucosa, reduces blood cholesterol level; is an adrenal tonic, anti-allergic, anti-viral, laxative and anti-inflammatory. Used internally for cold, Flu,

94

bronchitis, dry and hawking cough, chesty coughs, asthma, gastric ulcers and gastric inflammation, hastens and aids recovery after steroid therapy. *Use with utmost caution in pregnancy, high blood pressure, liver cirrhosis, while taking drugs based on digoxin. it must not be used in excess and for prolonged periods.*

Note : Most of the herbs, mentioned above, are used in tinctures and attentuations in Homeopathy but the leading symptoms, given above, may differ with that of Herbalism. If interested, the readers may refer to any standard book on Homeopathy, to derive additional information/knowledge, therapeutic uses of homeo drugs. Even creams, ointments and lotions can be prepared or purchased from the homeo chemists in ready-to-use form. As told earlier, most of the homeo medicines depend largely on various plants/herbs and/or their parts for medicinal purposes.

Leading Actions and Medicinal Properties of 12 Key Herbs

Yarrow

1. Urinary antiseptic
2. Anti-inflammatory
3. Checks and stops bleeding
4. Promotes and induces sweating
5. Blood Vessel relaxant

Marshmallow

1. Heals wounds faster
2. Diuretic
3. Expectorant
4. Soothing

Meadowsweet

1. Induces and promotes sweating
2. Mild urinary analgesic
3. Diuretic, promotes urinary flow
4. Antacid, soothing to the stomach and calms the digestive system & digestion
5. Anti-inflammatory and anti-rheumatic
6. Promotes and induces sweating

Pot Marigold

1. Heals wound quickly
2. Astringent
3. Antomicrobial
4. Anti-inflammatory

Agrimony

1. Bile stimulant and digestive
2. Diuretic
3. Heals wounds faster
4. Astringent

ST. John's Wort

1. Sedative and anti-depressant
2. Astringent and Anti-Viral
3. Slightly analgesic
4. Anti-inflammatory

Chamomile

1. Carminative and Sedative
2. Prevents Vomiting
3. Bitter
4. Antiseptic and Anti-bacterial
5. Anti-inflammatory

Vervain

1. Sedative and relaxant
2. Uterine stimulant
3. Promotes milk-flow in Nursing women
4. Promotos sweating
5. Bile stimulant

Thyme

1. A stimulating tonic
2. Expectorant
3. Anti-viral, antiseptic and anti-microbial.
4. Antispasmodic and Carminative

Wood Betony

1. A bitter but digestive remedy
2. Astringent, mild sedative and tonic
3. Tones up cerebral circulation

Rosemary

1. Circulatory and heart tonic
2. Antiseptic and Anti-bacterial
3. Antidepressant
4. Tonic and Nervine stimulant
5. Carminative

Lavender

1. Anti-depressant and Nervine Tonic
2. Topical circulatory stimulant
3. Carminative and Anti-spasmodic
4. Antiseptic and Anti-bacterial

The above-mentioned 12 herbs, are known as 'Twelve Key Medicinal Herbs'

Use of Essential Herbal Oils For Various Disorders and Aromatherapy

Basic Factors

Essential oils, derived from herbs, can be utilised in the following forms.

1. Use of essential oils with vaporisers
2. Using essential oils with water
3. Massage
4. Aromatic Relaxation
5. Tonic, Aromatic skin care
6. For relieving pains and aches
7. For Aromatic skin care
8. For inducing sound, reposeful and refreshing sleep.

9. Aromatic Ambience

10. Use of Essential oils with applicators

It is a myth that all essential oils are costly and not affordable by majority of people. This statement is partly true, for the simple reason that most of such oils are well within reach of most of us, while a very few can only be afforded by affluent and rich gentry but, all the same, multiple benefits, accruing after use of essential oils to dispel various disorders, cannot be negated nor denied. There is hardly any (herbal) cream/ointment where oils of plants are not used. It is maintained that, by weight, gold is cheaper than rose oil but it is also true that gold cannot dispel your ailments but rose oil can. If you purchase a set of phial of these oils, you won't be spending more than what you spend while feting and entertaining your relatives/friends in a restaurant. See the gains you derive by spending on your party and essential oils. When it is the question of health, money factor is hardly of any consequence. Remember, if you are in disposed, you won't be able to enjoy your food also.

Before drying essential oils, a few cogent factors and facts need to be kept in mind, viz.

(i) Essential oil is a spirit-like substance, especially if it evaporates in the air.

(ii) Oils derived from sunflowers or olives are turgid and greasy substances which do not evaporate in the air, hence those are not volatile.

(iii) Scent of essential oils is extremely strong if sniffed neat and directly.

(iv) Some essential oils help to revive consciousness quickly, say if a person falls unconscious, he can be revived.

(v) Essential oil is not, at all, oily, but makes your eyes water as soon as smelled or sniffed.

(vi) If a drop of an essential is put on the tissue, the drop will disappear quickly.

(vii) Fragrant oils are oily, give out a pleasing smell and do not evaporate as essential oils do.

(viii) Carrier oils are used as vehicles in which essential oil is mixed so as to make the oil massage more effective and to hasten penetration. You can easily use mustard, coconut, oil as 'Carrier Oils' for massaging purposes, hence there are pressed vegetable oils which are said to be safer and better. Such oils are known as 'Professional Carrier Oils' or 'Fixed Oils'.

Use of Essential Oils with Vaporisers

In order to yield optimum benefits, pour water in a utensil which should be heated on burner/stove/candle. Main aim and purpose is to generate requisite heat so that molecules of essential oils reach out to the room's atmosphere. Pour a few drops in the hot water and let the vapours reach out to every nook and corner of the room. Purpose, behind such exercises, is to drive out bad/foul smell from the room so as to make it a better living, germ-free, foul odour free room. It will have soothing, refreshing, deodorizing, fragrant effect. Use of light-bulb ring is merely a luxury—it may have aromatic effect, but no therapeutic effect, so to say. Such methods create moods, freshen the air, make room environment more attractive to lovers, visitors, friends, and drive away undesirable germs. Geranium, Sandalwood, Patcholi. Oils may be used direct onto the skin as perfumes.

Use of Essential Oils with Water

You can easily dispel your fatigue, revive your doomed spirits, get red of foul body odour by dropping a few drops of essential oils in lukewarm bathing water. Your tired nerves and muscles can be soothed, pain dispelled, gives freshing and amiable look to your skin if you use such oil mixed with water. You can use a few drops in sauna bath, to boost up your spirits.

Steam inhalation is another excellent source. Put in a few drops of essential oil (s) in a boiling pan or kettle and cover your head and face with a tea-towel and inhale the medicated vapours which will relieve you of chest congestion, trapped phlegm, nasal congestions and colds. It will also serve as a facial provided your skin is not highly sensitive to any of the ingredients. If you feel discomforted by steam vapours, you can sprinkle a 4-5 drops of the requisite essential oil on your hanky or shaving towel and inhale the smell to get rid of the said disorders, though your nose and mouth will be in direct touch with the oil, yet your eyes will remain safe. Such essential oils can also boost up your doomed spirits, give you a 'lift' and relieve your anxiety.

Massage and Essential Oils

Old persons practised and propagated the efficacy and benefits of massage and were so much impressed by the massage techniques that it formed an essential part of their health-care program. They used to assert that if you massage 200 gms of mustard oil into your body, it would give you benefits of ingesting one Kilogram of desi ghee (clarified butter). Affluent and health-conscious rich persons engage even permanent masseurs for the purpose. In India hands are used for massaging but in 'Kerala massage' feet are also used for the same person. The author once suffered from extreme pain in the cervical portion, shoulder blades. He was treated by a sports coach who massaged the affected portions and adjoining areas and, surprisingly, relieved the author of all pains within 4-5 minutes which was nothing short of an miracle.

In western world there are fine techniques of massage such as

— Stroking
— Patting
— Knuckling
— Rubbing and
— Squeezing

Use following precautions in relation to massage —

• Do not massage when a person is not fit either mentally or physically or both.

- Never massage on bleeding, open, broken, weeping organs of the body.

- Do not massage with an oil if someone has known allergy to either vehicle or essential oil or both.

- If someone is under influence of drugs and/drink (alcohol) he/she should never be administered any type of massage.

- It is always better to check-up with the attending doctor whether the patient is susceptible/allergic to any aromatic oil or whether such oil will interact with other drugs & used internally or locally.

Stroking

It is a technique of pull or push motion. Heart should be taken as centre of the body. A masseur can use pressure while he is pulling or pushing towards the heart but, while stroking away from the heart, he should use only the high test touch. Stroking should be used in-between other methods of massage, or else it can be started or begun with all other techniques of massage.

Patting

Patting should be done with finger tips so as to induce stimulation to smaller areas. This technique is the minimum used technique.

Knuckling

Here hands are clenched in very light fists when gentle circular movements are made by using knuckles of top joints of hands.

Rubbing

Rubbing used to generate heat in the body as two hands are rubbed or feet are rubbed with hands or else some oil or object is rubbed on the body to generate heat. Better results can be expected if body/parts are massaged faster and harder. Rubbing is an old Indian method of massage

Squeezing

This is known as 'squeeze and let go' technique which is performed powerfully with both hands. The masseur has to use plenty of force and effort in order to leave visible impact on the massaged person.

Advantages of Massage

Here the point under discussion is primarily herbal oil/ massage which is a part of general massage and the advantages derived from massaging which are as follows :

- It relieves high blood pressure but, more particularly, it keeps blood pressure within normal confines.

- It removes indigestion, constipation, flatulence, thereby improving general digestion, by invigorating the relative organs.

- Relieves stress related disorders like headaches and insomnia.

- It increases and tones up muscles, joints, increases flexibility and mobility, hence of great value in 'back-pain', arthritis, body pain and fatigue.

- It affords relief from all types of aches and pains, stiff joints etc.

- Removes depression and anxiety.

- Activates cardiac rhythm and increases the efficiency of heart.

- Improves supply of oxygen and nutrients to body tissues and enhances skin-tone.

- It stimulates lymphatic system, improves elimination of chemical wastes from the body, such as lactic acid that often leads to stiffness and pain in the muscles and joints.

Massage is not a therapeutic method to cure or treat any disorder. It is simply a method to accelerate, rejurvenate, repair the wasted tissues, rebuild energy and enhance functional mobility of body organs. If the body has been properly massaged and more emphasis is laid on more fatigued and ailing body parts, it is natural to feel lighter, painless and happier after the massage. Expertise and acumen of the masseur bes in his manipulative techniques.

It is wrong to conclude that massage is possible through application of oils on the body and their absorption by hand manipulation. This is simply one aspect of massage therapy. There are many other techniques practised the word over, such as Acupressure, Reflexology, Rolfing, Shiatsu, Indian Panchakarma and head massage, sweedish/western massage, facial massage. Ingam Reflex method of reflex massage, Thai massage, Aston Pattering, Metaphoric technique in Naturopathy, polarity therapy etc. In India it is generally opined that the masseur benefits more than the patient whom he massages, though it shouldn't be construed the patient doesn't get any benefit. We can derive a conclusion that if one is in a position of massaging by himself, he will derive optimum benefits.

Be careful not to massage your body under certain disordered body conditions detailed earlier. Massage is no substitute for all body ills nor is it a sure way to health, nor can it replace traditional system of medicine, but it well certainly help you to relax your body limbs, your body as a whole, dispel mental and physical fatigue, remove and aid in general body upkeep, do away with pains and aches, improve your general mobility, push up digestion, restore normally of bowels, improve your circulation and respiratory process and, above all, giving you a welcome feeling of well-being and betterment.

Use of Oils in Massage

Depending on type of ailment, oils may be added to light vegetable oil/talcum powder, after seeking a herbalist's expert opinion as to what kind of oil could be added to carrier oil, in order to get resignation from specific illnesses/disorder. A condensed list of therapeutic uses of oils is given below, *care must betaken to see that your skin is not allegic to smell and/ or local application of oil otherwise adverse reactions are likely to ensue.*

Clary Sage

Mental fatigue, Nervous tension, depression anxiety Premenstrual syndrome, menstraul pain, flatulence, indigestion.

Lavender

Flatulence, indigestion, colic, diarrhoea, high blood pressure, palpitation, breathlessness, headaches (especially nervous or/and tension headache), insect bites and stings, burns, acne.

German Chamomile

Allergic conditions pertaining to asthma and hay fever, acne, eczema, insomnia, headaches, flatulence, indigestion.

Rosemary

Muscular Aches and pains, Nervous tension, Premenstrual syndrome, headache, colitis, indigestion, flatulence, catarrh, congestion due to sinus,.

Tea Tree

Catarrh, Colds, Coughs, Thrush, Cystitis, insect stings/ bites, cold sores, Acne, Athlete's foot.

Sandalwood

Bronchitis, Laryngitis, Sore throats, Acne, Eczema, Cystitis, Insomnia, Depression.

Peppermint

Catarrh, headaches and Migraines caused by disgestive upsets and problems, Indigestion, flatulence.

Note : In certain individual carrier oil may suit one's body but essential oils may not or Vice Versa. *Unless suitability of* *carrier and essential oils has been clearly established, neither type of the oils should ever by used.*

Cautions :

1. German chamomile shouldn't be used in pregnancy. It may cause dermatitis in some cases.

2. Do not give peppermint to children below 12, and must not be used while Homeopathic treatment continues. Use in low duration.

3. If you are suffering from Epilepsy, high blood pressure and during pregnancy.

Above-mentioned cautions apply equally to oral/local use, in massage, inhalation, infusion.

I had read somewhere about massage with mustard oil. Swami Sivananda had advocated addition of pinch of salt to mustard oil so as to enhance its action and quicker absorption. In winter the oil should be slightly heated and then massaged. Next to mustard oil comes coconut oil which should be melted on slow fire in winter and massaged lukewarm. The Swami has not said anything about addition of salt thereto. In winter (Johnson's) baby oil or else bland olive oil is an excellent massaging vehicle for all the age-groups.

When full body is massaged, stress should be laid on all the parts equally, of course keeping in mind tenderness of some specific parts. If there is pain and swelling anywhere in the body, the affected part should be massaged very gently. If there is no allegic reaction, do not forget to mix 4-5 drops of essential oil with the carrier oil so as to enhance its efficacy. No bleeding, open, punctured area of the body should ever be massaged. A little care will bestow immense yield but even slight carelessness can dispel doom-hence always use your discretion.

Aromatic Relaxation

Relaxation simply means a state of tension-free mind when both remain reposed, quiet and calm. Use clary sage for anxiety,

107

depression and mental fatigue, and Rosemary also for the above-mentioned symptoms, apart from headache (even tension headache) Sandalwood will remove insomnia by inducing sound sleep and also relieve depression. Oil of these herbs can be used in infusions, teas, in carrier massage oils.

Tonic Effects of Herbs

Purpose of these herbs is to boost energy levels in the body and also push up general well-being. Use undermentioned herbs to derive the specific salutary effects.

Gotu Kola : It is also called Indian Pennywort or Centella Asiatica whose aerial parts are used to ward off old age and counter most of the aging problems. It is also helpful for improving failing memory. In times of stress and anxiety use its tea. It is quite bitter, but is an excellent digestive tonic, a diuretic, relaxant and laxative and takes away fatigue.

Ginseng : It is of two varieties, Siberian and Korean, though the latter is more commonly used but their therapeutic value is almost identical. Root of Siberian Ginseng is used. It is antiviral, anti-stress, an adrenal stimulant, an aphrodisiac, reduces blood sugar level, is a circulatory stimulant and immune stimulant.

It provides extra energy to the body to stand up and cope with run-up to a stressful state, and can assist in chronic fatigue syndrome. As for ladies, it is a preferred choice as compared to Korean Gising. It also counters effects of radition and chemotherapy treatment.

Korean Ginseng (Also called King Plant, Ren Shen, Panax Ginseng) is more suitable to men than women, though doesn't cause any harm to the latter. Its root is used for medicinal uses. It is a heart tonic, an apbrodisiac, tonic, immune stimulant, reduces cholesterol and blood sugar. Since it is rich in steroidal compounds, which are similar to human sex hormones, hence its use as an aphrodisiac. It is a useful tonic in winter and also aids in faster recovery from chest problems. It is a boon for men who are sexually weak and are unfit to perform sex act. Avoid using caffein while you are using Korean Ginseng.

Damiana : (Curzon, Turnea Diffusa VER Aphrodisiac). It is mood elevator and enhancer, revives mood, is an aphrodisiac, antidepressant and diuretic. For medicinal purposes its aerial parts are used. It is a useful tonic in convalescence, helps in prostatic and menstrual problems, is a stimulant.

Dang Gui : (Chinese Angalica, Dong Quai, Polymorpha VAR, Sinuses). Its root is used for medicinal purposes. It is a blood tonic, an analgesic, uterine stimulant, laxative, anti-spasmodic and circulatory stimulant and is widely used as a women's tonic, particularly after child-birth. *It must not be used during the period of pregnancy.* It is also used to treat various menstrual problems and anaemic states.

Reishi : (Red lacquered Bracket Fungus, Ganoderma Lucidem, Ling Zhi). It is anti-viral, anti-tumour, anti-bacterial, expectorant, sedative, reduces high blood pressure, is an immune stimulant. It is a Choicest energy tonic for enjoying long life. Used to advantage in many liver disorders, including hepatitis. It is an effective tonic for the elderly persons and the over-anxious ones. It is said to lower cholesterol and blood sugar levels.

Note : Though in the said list and details of sex tonic herbs essential oil is not used, yet I have taken liberty to include these herbs for the benefit of the readers lest requisite informatory knowledge is lost to them.

To Relieve Pains and Aches : Pains and aches not only disturb body but they also disturb the mind of the sufferers. Since human life came into being, all systems of medicines have been trying relentlessly to alleviate gravity and intensity of pain and ache. Herbal remedies affect aches/pains in the following menners, as they—

(i) Rid the body of irritant toxins

(ii) Repair the damaged tissues and

(iii) Improve circulation

(iv) Do not act as superficial analgesics

Following methods may be tried, keeping in view a patient's reaction or allergy to certain ingredients.

For Arthritis and Rheumatism Related Pains/Aches

Yarrow	-	20 gms
Celery seeds	-	20 gms
Dried Meadowsweet	-	60 gms
Dried Elder berries	-	50 gms
Dried Burdock Root	-	50 gms

Mix yarrow, celery and meadowsweet and prepare a decoction by adding 15 gm berry to 750 ml of water. Now strain on to yield 10 gm of the herbal mixture in a teapot and infuse for 10 minutes. Normal dose being a cupful of tea thrice daily-Before a dose is taken, the mixture should be reheated.

(ii) To relieve Muscular Pains and Aches

Essential oil of Lavender Oil ⎤ infused in 20 ml
Essential oil of Rosemary Oil ⎟ of St. John's Wort
Essential oil of Thyme Oil ⎦

Take a sterilized bottle (dark bottle of glass) and add all the above ingredients to St. John's Wort oil, and shake well. Take ½ TSP of the said mixture of oils on your palm and rub the same with the other hand and massage over the aching and painful parts quite gently, with a soft hand. Such local application may be repeated twice daily. It will ease muscular pain & stiffness.

(iii) To get rid of damage caused by previous injuries to joints and adjoining areas (in case of arthritic joints) rub cream/oil of comfrey to the affected joints. If you really wish to gain fullest advantages from this local application, you should eliminate animal foods/products and carbohydrates from your diet, as these foods leave acid wastes in the body, thereby aggravating arthritic and rheumatic conditions.

(iv) Devil's Claw's (taken in capsule form, 500/600 mg thrice daily perdose, for at least, six weeks) used in arthritic and rheumatic pains and aches is an age-old remedy in above conditions and their curative effects have been substantiated by prolonged research.

Devil's Claw is an effective and powerful anti-rheumatic, anti-arthritic, anti-inflammatory and analgesic agent, but *must not be used in pregnancy.*

Note : *Reference may be made to relevant pages in this book for cautions which prohibit use of the said drugs under certain physical conditions where they can prove harmful, counter-productive and reactive.*

Aromatic Skin Care.

Skin envelopes our all body organs and the first part of a body that is viewed by a viewer is skin. When we talk of skin-care, we imply face, neck, hands and feet, out of which face is the barometer of our expressions, reactions and sensitivity, hence ladies always accord top most priority to face, followed by hair, hands and feet. If whole body is massaged, the masseur will massage from top to toes. It may be remembered that stress free mode of life is a prerequisite for skin-care.

First of all, dip a towel in hot/lukewarm water and rub over face hands and feet and wipe out and cleanse these parts so that pores of skin get opened and cleaned. Mix rose water, lemon water, glycerine, a few drops of lavender oil (if well tolerated and not reactive). Apply over face, hands and feet. This is meant for summer's dry and hot winds but during winter and chilly weather, add a TSP of almond oil so that dryness and roughness of skin could be removed. Let the solution remain applied for an hour or so whereafter the apart should be wiped with lukewarm water. *Do not use very hot water over face.*

Inducing Sound Sleep : Some illness discomfort, mental agitation, overwork generated physical fatigue or even an unknown and undetected factor could form basis of insomnia.

If you enjoy sound sleep, despite the presence of all/some of the said factors or/and without aid of tranquilising/sleeping tablets, alcohol, drugs, you are perhaps a lucky guy, for sleep is, by far, the best and most cost-effective tonic that is capable of taking away your mental and physical problems. Non-addictive sedative, herbs are decidedly a better source for inducing sound sleep. Length of sleep is no measuring rod for healthy and refreshing sleep. If you get up in a gayful, happy, refreshing mood after sleep, however short it might be, you will start your day with a better and cheerful way. Try following herbs, if you are not allergic to them.

Dried Lemon Balm	-	15 gms
Dried Skullcap	-	60gms
Dried Vervain	-	30gms
Dried Wood Betony	-	60gms

Mix these herbs and prepare an infusion (as described earlier under relevant heading) from 2 TSP to make one cup. You can take upto such 4 cups (maximum) in 24 hours to get rid of tension and stress. For insomnia use the following herbs.

Hops	-	30gms	Mix these herbs
St. John's Wort	-	30gms	and use infusion,
Dried Vervain	-	30 gms	as mentioned
Dried Skullcap	-	60 gms	above

Dose and frequency being the same as in case of anxiety. You may add some honey to sweeten the liquid (infusion) since hops are quite bitter.

Aromatic Ambiency : Diluted essential oils of rose, lavender, sandalwood etc. are frequently used for the purpose. Oil of Jasmine also falls under the same category. These oils should be used not as a matter of habit but of necessity, otherwise one may develop revulsion to all these oils. Rose oil is perhaps the costliest.

Caution : Due to allergies of various etiologies, some of you may show hypersensitivity to some/all of the essential oils. If you are sensitive to one ingredient and recepctable to another, this cycle may get reversed, that is you may not be sensitive to an ingredient today but may react to the same the other day. This situation is true of every individual, without any exception. Personal likes and dislikes play an important part in choosing or rejecting a particular oil/herb.

While using essential oil for sensual pleasures, be careful to use only that oil that pleases both the partners, or else it may set in a turn,-off and, thus spoil chances of a joyous meeting. As for skin is concerned, one must be extra cautious while applying any oil on the body locally. Frangrant oils are meant to enhance your pleasure and not to drive you away from the scene of love-making.

Herbal Kingdom

(A DETAILED ACCOUNT OF SOME GENERALLY AND COMMONLY USED HERBS FOR VARIOUS USAGES)

In this chapter only those herbs would be detailed which are commonly used for various purposes and are easily available and cost-effective also. Most of the herbs and their derivatives, described earlier, do not suit pocket of a common man and are available only at selected high-profile sales outlets, apart from being quite costly. But, despite all such factors, their efficacy and utility cannot be overlooked and denied. If your pocket does not permit you to buy costly herbs, you can easily substitute them with less costly herbs which, in many cases, have the same beneficial properties.

While using any herb for therapeutic uses, it must be ascertained which part of the herbal plant is to be used. It is rarely that a plant is used as a whole but it is quite often, that either leaves/flowers/fruits/rind, stem are used, whether singly or jointly. Remove dust, any other foreign matter clinging on to the plant's useable part, either by washing or dusting it.

Even the vegetables growing underneath the land or above it are used for medicinal uses, for instance garlic, onion, bitter gourd cabbage, etc. All the spices used in kitchen are also used in various eating delicacies and medicines. Hence, when we talk of herbs, it includes all fruits, vegetables also. Plant kingdom is too vast and varied and all the plants are not used for processing medicines, because some of them are poisonous and harmful, carry health harzards. Further, it may be noted that certain herbal plants can cause reactions and allergies to some persons, hence all such plants must be with utmost care, if at all required.

BELLERIC MYROBLAN (Bahera, बहेड़ा)
(Terminalia Beleria)

It is a large tree with large leaves, having small pale green (foul-smelling) flowers in simple egg-shaped spikes, brownish long fruits which are thickly covered with hair. Dried fruits of the tree are used as drugs in various preparations. This tree does not grow in dry regions but is quite commonly available in forests. Its herb is rich in tannin substances. It is quite bitter in taste.

Its curability lies in treating fevers, arresting bleeding/ secretion. It is one of the constituents of *Triphala* whose other two constituents being *Amla* (Embelica Myrobalan) and Harar (Chebulic Myrobalan). It relieves coughs, sore throat, eye disorders, chronic and obstinate constipation, and stomach disorders.

Cough and Sore Throat

It is a commonly used household remedy. Prepare a mixture of pulp of the fruit, adding salt, long pepper and honey and taken in a TSP dose 3-4 times daily. In order to get rid of catarrh and cough, cover its fruit with wheat flour and then roast, and then suck slowly.

Intestinal Worms

It helps to expel all types of intestinal worms, hence its reputation as an effective anthelmintic. Prepare powder of the pulp of ripe fruit and mix Butea (Palash) seeds. If you take a TSP, 2-3 times daily, with warm water, desired results can be achieved.

Indigestion and Diarrhoea

Prepare an infusion/decoction from 1-3 gms pulp of this fruit, adding some salt to it. It would dispel disorders of loose motions and indigestion.

Watering From the Eyes

This is also known as 'lachrymation' in which condition profuse water flows down the cheeks due to poor performance of tear-drainage system. Though this not a serious disorder, yet it calls for medical aid. Its herb can be applied over (not in the eyes) eyes for soothing and curative effects.

Chronic Constipation

Its ripe and dried fruit causes constipation, while half ripe is used for removal of chronic and obstinate constipation. You can simply suck small pieces of its half ripe fruit.

It is also useful in fever, leprosy, piles, drops, dry and hawking cough but, when sucked, it may cause dryness and bitter taste in the mouth.

BUTEA (Butea Monosperma, Palash, पलाश)

It is a well known tree in our country whose flowers are scarlet and orange coloured. It is a tree of medium height, having compound leaves which fall in February/March in dense clusters on leafless branches and then it appears as if the tree is on fire. Its fruits are flat pods, having single seed in each fruit. Its trees are found abundantly in western and central India's forests. Its red-coloured gum (called Butea gum of Bengal Kine) is very rich in tannic and gallic acids. Its seeds contain a yellow fixed oil (called Kino-tree oil/Mudooga) which contains large quantity of water soluble albuminoid and resin. Its fresh seeds also contain Lipolytic & Proteolytic enzymes, whereas its flowers are replete with butren, buten, neteroside and glucosides, apart from number of fatty acids which have been isolated from its oil.

For its healing and properties seeds, leaves and gum are used. Its leaves have aphrodisiac and tonic qualities, apart from curing bleeding and secretion.

Diabetes

Use its powdered leaves to reduce blood sugar. It also is useful when urine is heavily loaded with sugar which condition is known as 'Glycosuria'.

Sore Throat

Boil leaves of butea in water and prepare a decoction for being used as a mouth-wash in septic and congested throat infection.

Skin Problems

Its seeds are used in various skin disorders like ulcers, tumours, piles, boils, pimples, swellings and itch (particularly the one so often experienced by the washermen), eczema. Its seeds should be ground to powder form and then mixed with lemon juice and applied over the itching side and/or applied in ringworm infections. Use the crushed seeds to kill worms, insects in wounds. Prepare its hot poultice of its leaves for local application over boils, ulcers, pimples, piles (tumourous variety).

Leucorrhoea

It is also known as 'The Whites' or 'White Discharge' from the vagina. Prepare an infusion or decoction for being used as a vaginal douche.

Intestinal Worms

Its seeds kill round and tapeworms for which, mix seeds

(750 mg to 1 gm) with honey and take thrice daily for 3 days. Take a TBSP of castor oil on the 4th day to evacuate and cleanse the bowels.

Loose Motions (Diarrhoea) and Dysentery

For the above disorders, its gum is used but, due to its mild effect, it is considered more suitable for women and children of delicate nature. Its usual dose ranges from 3 decigrams to 2 gms, adding a few decigrams of aromatics to the butea gum in the form of infusion/decoction, or else use either of these for a rectal enema.

Difficult Urination

This disorder is technically known as 'Retention of urine', where there is difficulty in passing urine, which condition can be mollified by giving fomentation over pubic region.

BISHOP'S WEED (Trachyspernum Ammi Omum or Ajawain, अजवायन)

It is an annual shrub with fine soft hairs, having many branched leafy stems. Its fruits are greyish, minute and shaped like an egg. its seeds are used in Indian, Greek, Unani and Egyptian systems of medicines. It is widely cultivated in countries like India, Afghanistan and Iran.

100 gms of seeds of Ajwain give 363 calorific value and contain Protein : 17.10%, Fat : 21.8%, Fibre : 21.2%, carbohydrates : 24.6%, Minerals : 7.9%, and Moisture : 7.4%, besides vitamins & minerals like Iron, Carotene, Calcium, Phosphorus, Niacin, Riboflavin, Thiamine and some other minerals. Due to presence of thymol in its essential oil, it is used abundantly in medicines and oil is obtained by steam distillation of its crushed seeds.

Therapeutic Uses : Flatulence, Indigestion, Polyuria, Asthma, Bronchitis, Common Cold, Toothache, various other Gastro-intestinal orders, Cardialgia, Ear-ache, Pain in throat, Arthritic and Rheumatic Pains, Migraine, and also used as an aphrodisiac. It is also widely used to enhance virility and premature ejaculation, besides use of its greyish brown seeds and fruits in spice.

Digestive Disorders

— Prepare pickle of lemon, rock salt, bishop's weed (seeds), finely sliced small pieces of fresh garlic. Let the contents remain in a glassware or chinaware for about 7 days after which a few slices can be eaten with meals daily. It will dispel colic, flatulence, sour and bitter eructations, dyspepsia, loss of appetite. It is also an anti-spasmodic pickle.

— To remove flatulence and constipation take ¼ TSP of Ajwain and ½-1 TSP of Powder of Harar (Belleric Myrobalan) which should be taken with lukewarm/hot water at bed-time. To make it more effective, add some rock salt, powder of black pepper, dry ginger powder also.

— Soak Ajwain seeds in lemon juice and take it daily to improve digestion.

— Where wind is trapped in the stomach, there is also flatulent colic, indigestion and other dyspeptic disorders, seeds of Bishop's weed may be given in the form of volatile oil (1-4 drops) in lukewarm water, or else simply taken (seeds) with black salt, ginger juice (½ TSP).

Urinary Disorders

— Take 2 gms of ajwain with 3 gms of sugar candy thrice a day with water to get rid of strangury and tenesmus

— If excess quantity of urine is passed frequently, 1 TSP of ajwain with equal quantity of jaggery (Gur) should be given (with water or still better with coconut or barley water). It will also remove burning sensation in the urine.

Respiratory Disorders

— To expel trapped and/or dried up phlegm, give seeds with butter milk. Its seeds are also useful in bronchitis.

— In acute laryngitis and influenza chew a garlic clove with a, pinch each of common salt and ajwain seeds.

— If chest is tied with hot seeds, as a poultice, it will lessen sputum.

— Chew ajwain and betel leave, at night, before sleeping to control and cure dry cough.

— When nostils are congested and blocked up by thick mucus, inhale crushed seeds, tied up in a piece of cloth, or else boil a TSP of seeds in water and inhale vapours (suitable for adults, in particular)

— Powdered seeds, a TSP of honey, ginger juice should be mixed and licked 3-4 times daily (1 TSP dose).

— If a small bundle of seeds, couched in a small piece of cloth and kept near pillow, it will relieve nasal congestion.

Rheumatic and Arthritic Pains

— Massage ajwain oil on affected parts-it will relieve neuralgia also.

— Prepare paste of seeds and apply locally over painful parts (in the form of poultice) to quell pain. If the skin is hypersensitive, powdered seeds may be mixed with coconut or mustard oil and then applied locally by gentle massage.

Migraine : Seeds should be sniffed or smoked. It will also provide relief in delirium.

Female Disorders

Leucorrhoea : Soak 125 gms of seeds in an earthen pot overnight, and prepare a paste-to be taken with water.

Infertility : Prepare paste of 25 gms of seeds, as directed above, and add sugar candy (125 gms) and start taking the contents from I day of menses, or ajwain can be used with chapatis and mixed with pulses (green grain-Moong Ki Dal) and eaten as a normal part of diet.

Menstrual Problems : Menstrual blood flow can be brought under control by taking 5 gms powder of ajwain.

A Post-Natal Tonic : Wash ajwain seeds and dry under shade, add Desi ghee, sugar or raw sugar and fry, with adding sooji. Take 1-2 TSP daily with milk, or take ground ajwain with jaggery—it will relieve back-ache, cleanse the uterus, stimulate digestion, increase appetite and impart strength to the body.

Whooping Cough : Ground seeds of ajwain (20 gms) and prepare a paste by adding black salt (5 gms) and honey (60 gms). Usual dose being ¼ to ½ TSP of for children and 1 TSP for adults—3-4 times daily.

Urinary Stones : Stones in bladders and kidney can be broken and expelled by taking 3-4 gms (raw) seeds of ajwain daily. It will also relieve flatulent colic.

As a Deodorant : It may look to be surprising and unbelievable that ajwain is a decodorant par excellence, as it kills cockroaches, insects and germs, and also purifies the air. Keep a TSP so in a piece of cloth and tie the same. It may be kept in a cup-board, near the barables, and at other places where insect/germs/cockroaches are already present or suspected to appear/reappear.

ANISEED (Pimpinella anisum, Vilayati Saunf)

Anise belongs to celery family and is an annual culinary herb and its fruit is known as 'Aniseed' which is an important part of every kitchen. It has a pleasant taste and an agreeable odour. It does not easily grow in tropical low lands, as it requires plenty of warmth and sunshine.

It contains essential oil, ash, starch, choline, sugars, plenty of protein, crude fibre. Chief constituent of aniseed oil is Anethole that imparts it pleasant and characteristic flavour. Its oil also contains chavicol, methyle, some amounts of p methoxyphenol acetone, terpenes. It carries high medicinal properties and has been in use, since long, in India, Europe, Mexico, Greece and Rome, Egypt, Asia Minor, due to its multiple uses.

If aniseed is boiled for too long it is liable to get divested of its essential oil and digestive properties due to heating/boiling process.

Therapeutic Uses

Digestive Disorders

It expels wind from the stomach and can be added to pepper, cumin and ginger (in equal quantities) and taken a TSP with water after meals.

It can be used also as an infusion. Mix a TSP of aniseed to a cup of boiling water, for being kept overnight. The clear fluid should be mixed with honey-1 TSP to be taken daily. It will remove gurgling in the abdomen, remove indigestion, prevent fermentation and gas formation in the bowels & stomach.

Insomnia

Add a TSP of aniseed to 400 ml of water, adding some tea to it. Let it simmer for fifteen minutes, and then strain (when the liquid quantity is reduced to 1/3rd quantity), adding hot milk and honey to it—it should be better taken at bed-time or sipped after meals.

Cure & Prevention of Cataract

Progression of cataract can be delayed for a fairly long span, or even cured by taking 5 gm aniseeds in the morning and evening or prepare powder from equal quantity of coriander seeds and aniseed, adding equal quantity of unrefined sugar to it. 10 gms of this mixture may be taken in the evening and morning.

Sundry Uses

To relieve flatulence anise oil is used as an aromatic carminative. For its flavoring quality its oil is for mouth washes and in dental preparations, in addition to for flavoring cakes, sweets, curries, biscuits and cookies.

For its insecticidal properties, it is used (externally) to kill vermin, lice and mites.

ARJUNA (TERMINALIA ARJUNA, KAHU)

Arjuna tree is indigenous to India, Srilanka and Myanmar (Burma), and grows mainly on marshy lands/water channels. Its bark is replete with large quantities of calcium and very small amounts of tannin, aluminium and magnesium, apart from containing Arginine (a crystalline compound), arjunetin, lactone, colouring matter, sugars and essential oils. Vaghabhatt, Chakra eulogised it for its cardiac efficiency and curability. It is used in homeopathy (in the form of mother tincture) and in Ayurveda in the form of Arisha and powder form (either alone or in combination with other medicinal ingredients). It is a cardiac tonic of high quality, arrests bleeding and/or secretion, promotes flow of bile, heals wounds faster and removes calculi (stones) from the urinary system, and also mollifies intensity of fever. Its bark is used for therapeutic uses.

Heart Problems

It stimulates action of heart, stops heart future and dispels dropsy. Modern practitioners use it as a heart tonic and stimulator of cardiac efficiency. Prepare a decoction from its bark and use with milk or else 1½ TSP of its powder may be put in tea/milk, or 0.75 to 2 gms powder mixed with honey.

Contusions/Fractures

Use ½ TSP of finely ground powder of bark with honey

and lick it 2-3 times, to help the bones gain strength and sturdity, consequent upon some fracture.

Acne

Prepare an ointment by mixing finely powdered bark with honey and apply it over acne eruptions. *It is said to be a successful treatment in acne.*

Aphrodisiac Properties

If powder of bark is taken, regularly with milk for 2-3 months or till improvement sets in, it will prove as an effective sex stimulant.

Asthma

The undermentioned treatment should be carried on the night of full moon. Prepare a dish from condensed milk sugar and rice to make a palatable kheer and put in an open bowl which should be covered with a thin muslin cloth and exposed to moonlight, making sure that the moonlight falls directly on the processed dish. Sprinkle 10-12 gms of powder of the arjuna bark over it and eat early next morning, but the patient must not sleep upto twelve hours after consuming the dish. This is said to be an effective and curative device in case of even chronic Asthma.

EMBLIC MYROBALANS (AMLA)

It maintains balance amongst three humors (Doshas) of wind, bile and phlegm (Vayu, Pitta and Cough) and effectively controls digestive problems, invigorates mental and physical activities, strengthens heart (cardiac muscles) builds up and sustains defence mechanism, improves eye-sight, imparts lustre and natural glow to hair and body, is an important constituent of famous 'Triphala' compound, and is a store-house of Vitamin 'C'. If used regularly or on prolonged basis, it is capable of prolonging life span. In addition to Vitamin-C, it also contains calcium, iron, protein, gallic and tannic acids, sugar, phosphorus, carbohydrates etc.

Curative Properties

Tonic for Heart, Eyes and Memory

— Wash eyes daily, in the morning, with amla water, soaked in water and drink the water to improve eyesight and remove constipation.

— Mix equal quantity of amla powder and black Til to honey/ghee (Desi) to improve mental and physical weakness.

— Mix ½-1 TSP of amla juice or powder with honey and take it daily to impart strength & freshness to body.

— Taking one piece of amla jam (Murabba) with milk (without sugar) will strengthen eye-sight, have tonic effect on heart, sharpen intellect and strengthen the body, expel toxins from the body and improve defence machenism of the body.

— Burning sensation in the eyes and heaviness of the head of hair are massaged with the pulp of amla or soak triphala overnight in water and splash water over eyes to improve general health and vision of eyes.

— Weakness of body, heart and mind shall be dispelled by taking fresh amla juice in between taking of meals.

— Massage your head with amla oil to induce sound sleep and roughness of hair.

— Prepare a paste of Neelkamal, rose water, kumkum and dried amla to cure headache.

Urinary Disorders

— Apply, near the navel, paste of amla to cure many urinary problems.

— Mix amla powder (one gram) Haldi powder (Turmeric), honey, and pounded sugar candy and take it with milk/ plain water, to get rid of night discharge.

— If there is blood in the urine, mix pulp of fresh amla (10 gms) with honey.

Sundry Uses

— Fresh amla juice checks impurities in blood
— To check diabetes take amla juice with honey
— To check piles, soak 15 gms each of amla and henna (Mehandi) leaves in 400 ml water and let it remain soaked overnight. Next morning strain the contents and take in divided doses.
— 10 ml amla juice, mixed with equal quantity of honey, will control cough and also help to expectorate phlegm.
— Mix amla powder to Jasmine oil and rub over those body parts where there is itching.
— Insert 2-4 amla juice drops into each nostril to cure bleeding from nose (Epistaxis)
— Dehydration can be controlled by taking a mixture of grape and amla juice but, in case of diabetics, grape juice should be substituted with honey.
— Prepare pickle of amla to improve digestion.

To get optimum benefits, use chayavanprash Avleha (Ashtawargayukta). One TSP may be taken daily with hot milk— an hour prior to retiring to bed at night. It is an excellent rejuvenator that aids in and improves general health, pushes general resistance of body to normalise all the humours, remove even habitual and/or obstinate constipation, improve cardiac function etc. It suits persons of all the age-groups and sexes.

CARDAMOM (Chhoti Elaichi)

It is second only to black pepper—the former called is 'queen' of spices and the latter called as 'king of spices' cardamom has pleasant aroma but is slightly pungent in taste. Its seeds are used to create sensation of warmth.

Cardamom is rich in calcium, iron, phosphorus, protein, carbohydrates, ether extract, crudes fibre and moisture. Its seeds contain volatile oil that contains constituents like terpineol, Terpinene, limonene, sabirene in the form of acetic and formic acids. For therapeutic uses it is used in—

126

Digestive Disorders

To increase appetite and soothe mucus membrane, to expel and remove gas and heart-burn. For which mix ground cardamom seeds with coriander, garlic and onion. For relieving indigestion and headache, cardamom should be used and boiled in tea. Its aromatic flavour relieves foul smell from mouth, hence used as a mouth freshener.

Urinary Disorders

Mix its finely powdered seeds with amla juice and banana leaf (to be taken thrice daily) in case of burning and scanty urination, cystitis, Nephritis and gonorrhoea.

Impotency and Premature Ejaculation

Boil 500-750 mg of powdered seeds of cardamom on milk and add honey to sweeten, for being taken at night to remove impotency and premature ejaculation but *excessive use of cardamom may prove even counter-productive, as it may cause impotency.*

Depression

Boil cardamom seeds in water/tea-it will remove depression, apart from imparting aromatic effect and odour to tea.

Hiccups

Prepare an infusion by boiling 2-4 pounded (whole) cardamoms alongwith 3-5 mint leaves—a cup of such preparation be taken to get rid of hiccups/hiccough.

It is used in betel-as a masticatory, and also used to flavour cakes, biscuits, pastries, curries, desserts and other culinary preparations. Oil of cardamom is frequently used to prepare tincutre, stimulants, for purposes of flavoring bitters and liquors.

Caution : *Those who are suffering from sub-mucus fibrosis (a state when mouth does not open fully due to stiffness of sub-mucus portion) must not use cardamom, at least orally, due to its extreme astringent effects. Moreover, whose mouth is sensitive, it may also be affected with stomatitis, hence use with utmost caution in the above mentioned disorders.*

CELERY (Apium Graveolens, Ajwain or Ajmod Ka Patta)

It is an important salad plant that consists of bulbous roots, green leaves and stem, and its leaves sprout (directly) from its fleshy roots. Its fruits are quite small, have dark brown colour and give out a peculiar smell when they are cut open. Its seeds are also brown in colour.

It is a basic food and is replete with vitamins, mineral & salts, containing protein 6.3%, Fat 0.6%, Minerals 2.1%, Fibre 1.4%, Carbohydrates 1.6% and moisture 88%, (Per 100 gms of edible portion). It contains a volatile oil, derived from its fruits, which resembles pale yellow colour and consists of anhydride, sedenolide, etc. Oils derived from celery fruits improve nervous weakness, and remove its causatives and tranqualise agitated nervous system. Celery seeds are often used with advantage to increase secretion/discharge of urine, relieve flatulence and used as an aphrodisiac. Ladies can get rid of frequent and unwanted pregnancies (as the seeds help to abort). Spasmodic disorders can also be corrected by using the celery seeds.

Gout, Rheumatism & Arthritis

Due to its high alkaline element, it does not permit acidity to set in. For gout and rheumatic disorders a fluid extract of its seeds should be used; as it also removes toxemia and hyperacidity.

Due to its high content of organic sodium, it helps to keep magnesia and lime in a solution form and does not allow them to deposit on and around the joints. For arthritis, juice (fresh) of its leaves and may be used.

Blood Disorders

Its high contents of iron and magnesium is an excellent food (tonic) for the blood cells. Juices of celery and carrot should be used in various conditions, such as haemophilia, anaemia, leukaemia, Purpura and Hodgkin's disease.

Nervous Disorders

Regular use of juices of celery and carrots is useful in Nervous afflictions, caused by degeneration of protective layer (cover) of the nerves. The said combination of juices restore the nervous afflictions of sensorium to its normal state.

Indigestion

Soak a TSP of celery seeds in a glass of buttermilk for 6-7 hours and contents, then, should be ground in the same liquid and given to get rid of indigestion.

General Debility

Weakness, due to malnutrition, can be removed by mixing a TSP of the powder (described above) with honey and taken twice daily.

Tendency to formation of Gallstones & Kidney Stones

Those who have the tendency to formation of stones in kidneys/gall bladder, should use it regularly to allay chances of reformation of stones for which celery juice/powder may be used.

Do not ever scrape or discard green portions of celery due to its valuable contents of vitamins; hence always use celery with its crispy (brittle) stalks and thick ribs. Celery can be used in the form of salads, (in its raw form), juice form, soups, and can be mixed with fruits and vegetables, cooked and taken with cream/butter, used to flavour sauces and stews.

GARLIC (Allium Sativum, Lahsum)

It is an erect biennial herb and belongs to onion family, each bulb containing 6-30 shallots (also called 'cloves') which are enclosed in a transparent, whitish, thick and glistering covering. It has been in use in medicines, food preparations, in oil form since 4500 B. C. Hippocrates strongly recommended its use in intestinal uses and therapeutic ingredients. It is grown almost all over the world.

It has volatile oil, (0.06%) mucilage (35%), starch and

albumen. In addition, it has carbohydrates 29%, Fat 0.1%, Protein 6.3%, Lime-0.03%, Mineral salts 1%, Phosphorus 0.31%, Iron 13%, sufficient quantity of vitamins A, B, and C, sugar, minerals (like manganese, albumin, lead, copper and chlorine).

Oil of garlic is obtained by distillation and is replete with various compounds of sulphur etc. Its colour is yellow or dark brown, odour repulsive, and taste pungent but possesses numerous medicinal properties. In food and medicines its peeled cloves are used.

Therapeutic uses

Garlic is one of the mostly used vegetations in medicines and its curative properties include cure of Fevers, Leprosy, Asthma, Arteria-Scleroris, High Blood Pressure, deafness. It is also used as a heart tonic, to expel intestinal worms, piles, cough and asthma, catarrhal disorders, T.B., bronchitis, paralysis, sore throat, rheumatism, cancer, skin and blood disorders, whooping cough, to heal ulcers and wounds, diphtheria etc. In addition, it is also used as an aphrodisiac.

It should be used carefully by those who have bilious tendency, whose liver is damaged or hypersensitive, whose skin is sensitive and digestive system is depraved, who get urticaria or any other skin eruption.

Some people do not use it due to its bad odour and pungent taste, though all of them are fully convinced of its food values and medicinal efficacy.

Asthma

Peel a pod of garlic, crush and boil the same in 125 ml of pure malt-vinegar which should be strained after cooling, adding equal quantity of honey, for being preserved in a bottle. To hasten quicker recovery, add decoction of fenugreek to 1-2 TSP of syrup (which is a single dose) which should be taken in the evening and at night before retiring to bed. It will reduce severity of asthmatic attacks.

Sundry respiratory disorders

Use garlic juice to dissolve trapped, tenacious and sticky mucus in the chest and sinuses, lungs and bronchial tubes. A decoction of garlic boiled in milk is a wonderful medicine for pulmonary gangrene, asthma tuberculosis and pneumonia. Put 1 gm garlic in 250 ml milk and add 1 litre of water and boil all the ingredients until reduced to ¼th quantity of decoction which should be taken 3-4 times in 24 hours.

Digestive Disorders

Garlic has the properties of stimulating peristaltic action of intestines, eliminating waste and poisonous matters from the body, expelling flatus (but not acidity), to activate lymph activity; help in secretion of digestive juice. It is an excellent remedy for infections and inflammations of stomach and intestines garlic oil eliminated (party) via our urine but is absorbed by alimentary tract. For all the side-effects, prepare on infusion of garlic (peeled and crushed) cloves in milk/water and take it regularly or till symptoms disappear.

Disorders like colitis, diarrhoea dysentery and worms can be treated by taking fresh garlic cloves (2-3) capsules (2-6), Garlic cloves (2-4) may be soaked in milk and kept overnight. These cloves can be taken as first thing in the morning (that is on empty stomach), or else reduce garlic cloves to pulp form and take with a TSP of honey.

Blood Disorders

It hardly matters how you use garlic but the only imperative being to use it regularly and use it for some time. Its herb is a great rejuvenator, as it helps to revitalise blood, stimulate blood circulation, promote intenstinal flora, is a bactericide and preventive of infection, and guards body against invasive, harmful external elements. To allay all the said complaints you can simply take garlic pulp or simply chew the cloves or else prepare its pickle by adding cumin seeds, black salt, lemon juice and ajwain seeds.

131

Cancer

Use garlic juices and extracts. Effects, after use of garlic, have proved that it can kill and destroy germs, reduce swelling, pain an to retard growth of cancerous tumour. Take 2-4 garlic cloves (peeled) daily and also apply garlic oil/juice over infected areas. If redness and itching persist, discontinue local application of garlic juice or oil.

Arthritis, Rheumatism, Lumbago

Garlic reduces inflammatory swelling, pain, stiffness. Take 2-4 shallots of garlic daily and apply garlic oil 2-3 times daily as local massage—the oil may be moderately heated in winter and hilly winds and then applied over painful and inflamed parts.

Skin Disorders

Take 3 garlic shallots daily (or else 3 garlic capsules daily) orally. Apply/raw garlic to cure acne, boils and pimples and blemishes. In rare cases, itching may surface, but, then, garlic juice may be applied with some vaseline/lotion. Garlic has strong capacity to purify blood. If garlic is rubbed over ringworm it will burn the area first and then enable the skin to peel off.

Whooping Cough

To abort recurrent and violent spells of cough, take 5 drops of garlic juice diluted in a TSP of water.

High Blood Pressure

Due to its property to ease spasm of small arteries, reduce pressure and tension, modify the heart rhythm and slow down pulse rate, relieve formation of gas, breathlessness, dizziness, take 2-3 garlic capsules/cloves daily to lower the raised blood pressure.

Caution : Whenever there is any oral/local reaction, use of garlic should be abandoned. Approach your physician for proper guidance and advice. Persons with sensitive and weak digestion, having jaundice and bile-related problems, hepatitis must use garlic, in any form, with physician's advice only. Overuse of garlic is also forbidden.

Aphrodisaic Effects

Garlic can cure weakness and debility caused by over indulgence in sex, in impotency, Nervous exhaustion of sexual incompetency, failing libido (particularly in old men). Prepare a kheer (dessert) from garlic cloves, as described earlier. Restrain your passions, so as to avoid coitus, until you are again sexually rejuvenated.

GINGER (Zingiber Officinale, Adrak)

Ginger plant is about 1.2ft high, having ground part is known as 'Rhizome' which is the edible portion of plant and is commonly known as 'Ginger-roots. When dried, it is called 'Saunth' or dried-ginger, root and fresh one is simply called 'Ginger' or 'Adrak', It has bitter taste and is pungent.

Therapeutic Properties

It is carminative, digestive, anti-flatulent, anti-pyretic, stomachic, invigorating, blood purifier. It is useful is cough, bronchial cough, nausea, it generates heat, expels sputum, checks purgation and griping. It is used often in medicines, in kitchen preparations, salads, with vegetable juices for seasoning and flavoring purposes.

It contains fat, volatile oil, crude liquid, Mucilage, resin, starch, Ash, Oleoresin gingerol or Gingerin. Its oil possesses aromatic odour, Ginger relieves muscular pain, and is counter-irritant, has aphrodisiac properties.

In western countries, ginger is widely used in breads (ginger-bread), pickles, soups, puddings, cakes, biscuits and is used in curries in the form of powder. Essential oil extracted from the rhizomes is used for perfumery and manufacturing essence. It is also used for medicinal and flavouring purposes. Its full pungency is preserved when oleoregin is extracted.

Certain regions in our country consume raw ginger after peeling and slicing into small pieces. If it tastes pungent and unpalatable, it should, first be used in cooked vegetables so as to develop taste.

Respiratory Disorders (including colds and cough)

Cut ginger into small pieces and then boil, add some honey or sugar to a cup of liquid and sip it or put in some ginger pieces in tea—it will remove cold, cough and congestion from lungs alongwith fever (by inducing profuse sweating). For asthma, bronchitis, influenza, whooping cough and T.B. of lungs, prepare a cupful of fenugreek decoction and add a TSP each of garlic juice and honey. It is an expectorant & diaphoretic of high order, as it will expel sputum and induce sweating, and avert recurrent episodes and bouts of cough.

Digestive Disorders

Its protective action is because of its properties of volatile oil, diastase enzyme and excessive salivary excretion. Mix a TSP each of fresh juices of mint and lime, ½ TSP of fresh ginger juice, and a TBSP of honey to get rid of indigestion (caused by fatty, spicy and heavy meals), dyspepsia, nausea, vomiting (due to biliousness), piles, jaundice, flatulence and flatulent colic, morning sickness etc. Even chewing a piece of fresh ginger after taking meals, will also have salutary effect on almost all digestion related disorders. If the taste is felt too pungent, you may add some black salt to it.

Soak finely sliced and chopped ginger pieces in lemon juice, adding black salt, ajwain (Bishop's weed), cumin seeds (powdered) and use it as a palatable pickle. If you wish to make it more effective, may you also add cloves of garlic (peeled) to the above ingredients—this preparation is a panacea for almost (all) the digestive upsets.

Pains and aches

Ginger is an excellent analgesic and is capable of curing

134

almost every type of pain/ache. Apply paste of ginger to temples and forehead to relieve headache (But ensure the ginger liquid does not fall into the eyes). It will also allay toothache, if applied over painful tooth. To seek relief from earache, 2-4 drops may be dropped in the painful ear.

Impotency

To cure impotency, premature ejaculation tone up sex organs, spermatorrhoea, etc. including seminal discharge (involuntary), take a half-boiled egg, ½TSP of juice of ginger and a TSP of honey, to be taken at night for 30-45 days to remove the said sexual disorders.

Menstrual Disorders

When irregular/painful menstruation is caused by taking cold bath or exposure to cold winds, boil a pounded piece of fresh of garlic in water. When it is infused fully, add some sugar and take such a dose, 3-4 times daily.

Paralysis

Grind Urad Dal (Black gram Dal) and prepare a paste which should be fried in pure ghee, adding sounth (dry ginger) powder and jaggery (Gur). Prepare laddus from this combination, and consume one laddu daily, or boil sounth in urad dal's water, and drink the resultant water to cure paralysis.

ONION (Allium Cepa, Piyaz)

Onion is a biennial herb that is grown, generally, annually. When crushed, all parts of onion produce a strong odour. Its plant is about a metre high, with succulent, cylindrical and conical leaves. Its leaves, bulbs are used for eating and medicinal purposes. Its colours are white, red or pale but for medicinal uses, its white variety is preferred. Its taste is both pungent and sweet.

Chemical Properties (Per 100 gms of edible portion)

Carbohydrates-11.6 to 13.2%, Protein-1.2-1.4%, Fat-0.1%,

Mineral salt-0.4-0.7%, Phosphorus-0.05-0.06% Calcium-0.04-0.18%, Iron-0.8-1.2 mgm, Vitamin B-40 I.U., Vitamin-C-11 mgm, Sugar-12%, Carotene-55 I.U., Thyme-120 mgm, Niacin-5 mcgm, Water-87% and evaporative oil that contains traces of sulphur.

Curative Properties

Increases vigour and vitality, acts as a stimulant, is a source of energy, expectorates phlegm, tones down raised heartbeat, prevents dyspepsia and flatulence, induces sleep. It is also used for disorders like arthritis, acne, Dental decay, hysteria, cholera, diarrhoea, jaundice, bleeding from nose, heart attack, menstrual upsets, insect-bites, baldness (alopecia), prevention stone formation, skin disorders, cold, cough, asthma, T.B. etc. In addition, it also is used in cases of high blood pressure, cholesterol rise in blood, arteriosclerosis.

Heart Attack and Blood Pressure (High)

Latest research has established, cardiac utility of onion. It is next only to garlic, in gradational medicinal efficacy which is due to presence of certain heart-friendly ingredients found in its essential oil. If one consumes 100 gms of raw onion daily, one can get rid of high blood pressure and coronary heart disease, as onion reduces high percentage of cholesterol in blood and also corrects thrombose.

Cholera

Add finely pounded seven black peppers' powder to 25 gms of onion juice and serve to the cholera patient. It will also allay restivity, thirst, nausea, vomiting and diarrhoea. Add little sugar or black salt, as per taste, to enhance effectivity of the recipe.

Respiratory Problems

Mix equal quantity of onion juice and honey (say -1-2 TSP of each) to cure cough, cold, influenza, bronchitis and common cold.

Skin Disorders

Onion has the property to stimulate blood circulation, apart from irritating it. Mix 1/3rd onion juice to ¾th quantity of water and wash wounds and body with it. To help drain out pus, apply a paste (prepared from onion, turmeric powder and mustard oil) to boils and abscesses.

Urinary Disorders

For diuretic effects, take onion juice with hot water or take 5-6 gms of onions and boil in water–when reduced to half the quantity, let it cool whereafter the same should be strained and given to the patient. To treat retention of urine, remove burning sensation, grate an onion and mix 60 gms of sugar to it–it will start free flow of urine.

Ear Disorders

Drop moderately heated juice of onion (2-3 drops) in the painful ear or drop 2-3 drops of fresh juice of onion by dipping it in a piece of cotton swab in it.

Miscellaneous Uses

1. Apply onion paste to heels, and also keep an onion in the pocket (while moving out in the heat) to cure and offset ill-effects of heatstroke–the latter device is useful as a preventive measure.

2. To promote growth of new hair, rub onion juice over the bald area on head.

3. Dental problems, like tooth pain, tooth decay and bacterial growths, can be offset and cured by eating a raw onion daily.

4. Infiltration of insects, mosquitoes can be dispelled if a piece of onion is tied near the lighting point.

137

5. Entry of snakes in the room can be prevented by keeping a white onion in the room.

6. Rub mixture of oil of sesammum and onion juice on painful and swollen arthritic joints.

7. To cure diarrhoea, apply onion paste on the navel region.

8. Bleeding from nose (Epistaxis) can be contained if a few drops are inserted into each nostril. It will also enable a person regain consciousness within a short time.

9. For dispelling hysterical attacks, let the patient inhale smell of a cut onion. Also rub his/her heels with a crushed onion.

10. Soak small cut onion pieces in lemon juice or vinegar and mix black salt and black pepper to it. Let the patient use it twice, in the form of medicine, to cure jaundice.

11. Use onion juice to reduce ill-effects of excessive intoxication.

CUMIN SEEDS (Cuminum Cyminium, Jeera, jeerak,)

It is one of the most commonly used condiments for preparing Dals, Vegetables, pickles, vegetarian and non-vegetarian preparations, and extensively used for processing Ayurvedic and Unani medicines.

Its chemical analysis reveals presence of Carbohydrates-35.5%, Protein 17.7%, Fat-23.8%, Crude Fibre 9.1%, moisture 6.2%, Mineral content 7.7% (per 100 gms) whose celorific value is 460. Its seeds also contain iron, sodium, potassium, vitamins A, B, & C, cumin seeds have 7.7% fat oil, gum and mucilage

8%, and Resin 13.5%. Its taste and odour exists due to, presence of essential oil that contains cumiral 56%–a misture of hydro-carbons, cymene or cymene Terpene.

Curative Properties

Its seeds, infusion, decoction and powder are used in disorders like diarrhoea, leucorrhoea, piles, urticaria, renal colic, common cold, chronic fever, increases milk in breasts of nursing mothers, amnesia, insomnia, swelling of hands & feet, post natal problems, removal of freckles and spots, insect-bites, and also used as an insect repellant, as a general tonic, stomach and digestion related problems, mouth infections and ailments.

Post Natal Problems

1. Jeera, Gur (Jaggary) helps the uterus to contract, and Jeera decoction restores uterus to its original position.

2. Take roasted (fried jeera (10 gms) with 50/100 gms to increase milk in the breasts, or jeera may be used in cooked vegetables or salads, may be used in cooked vegetables or salads or simply take jeera powder with water.

3. Take 1 TSP cumin powder and mix it with a cup of water so as to derive its antiseptic benefits and also contract the overies to their normal size.

Leucorrhea

Take ground roasted cumin to control leucorrhoea.

Piles

1. Mix roasted and unroasted cumin seeds (30 gms each) and reduce them to powder form–3 gms of this powder should be taken, twice daily, with water.

2. Take one TSP ground cumin with sugar-candy and water.

3. Boil fennel, corriander seeds and cumin seeds (one TSP each) and boil in 1 litre of water until one cup is left. Mix pure ghee to it and consume. It is very effective in curing bleeding piles.

Digestive Disorders & Diarrhoea

Cumin seeds remove atonic dyspepsia, flatulent colic, diarrhoea, eructations and belching, morning sickness, dyspepsia, malabsorption of food etc.—to quell all these disorders, decoct a TSP of cumin seeds, and when the quantity is reduced to a cup, add fresh juice of coriander, a pinch of black/rock salt-take a dose each after meals. It will also control diarrhoea.

Renal Colic

20 gms of cumin seeds, 12 gms of caraway seeds and 6 gms of black salt be ground together and then all these ingredients mixed with vinegar so as to prepare a mixture—this mixture (3 ml) can be taken even after every hour until colic subsides.

Urticaria and Pruritis (itching)

Take bath with water in which cumin has been boiled— it will cure urticaria and itching. It is also the method frequently applied by Naturopaths, while giving hot-bath in such complaints.

Freckles and Spots (Blemishes)

Wash your face with water in which cumin has been boiled—it will beautify the skin. Prepare a paste from black til, gound jeera and mustard oil, and add equal quantity of milk which should be applied on facial spots, freckles to impart natural glow and softness to face.

Chronic Fever

Boil Cumin seeds in (Cow's) milk and grind when dried. 3-4 gms of this powder may be taken with sugar-candy (Mishri) twice daily regularly, to cure chronic fever; or take cumin seeds/

powder (¾TSP of) with jaggery (Gur) twice a day for three weeks, without any break, for the same purpose.

Amnesia

This a state of dullness of memory. Mix powder of black cumin seeds with pure honey and lick it (twice daily) to get rid of this malady.

CARAWAY SEEDS (Siya Jeera)

Its plant is a biennial herb, having fleshy root and slander branched stems. Its dried fruits/seeds are hard and sharp to touch and are brown coloured, having aromatic flavour and pleasing odour, sharp taste, and impart a bit warm feeling within the mouth. Its seeds are used to bring bloom to young maiden's cheeks.

When chemically analysed, it shows substantial amount of protein, fat, carbohydrates, apart from iron, calcium, phosphorus, potassium, thiamine, niacin, riboflavin, Vittamins A and C, and ash. Its calorific value amounts to 465 (per 100 gms)

Its essential oil contains substantial quantity of carvone, strong flavour and odour, in appearance it is either pale yellow or simply colourless. The volatile oil contains a blend of terpene, traces of carvacrol, carvone and ketone.

Therapeutic Properties

For therapeutic purposes its roots, leaves and seeds are used to accelerate renal function/action, to activate glands, it scavangers the whole body and is, thus, regarded as a great cleanser and purger of toxins. Its oil is utilised (in medicine) to relieve flatulence and also used to correct griping and nausea symptoms caused due to use of certain other drugs.

Digestive and Stomach Disorders

Add a TSP of caraway seeds to tea water (one litre) and boiled. When reduced to 300 gms, it should be allowed to simmer on very slow fire for 15-20 minutes, whereafter it should be strained and sipped or lukewarm hot. It will remove flatulent colic, flatulence, offset bad effects of certain toxins and medicines. Instead, its volatile oil can be used for allaying said disorders.

Hookworms

Carvone (isolated from its oil) is an excellent worm-killer (anthelmintic), but is a specific remedy to expel hookworms from intestines.

Scabies

Mix small amount of oil (say 25%) to 75% quantity of castor oil and take orally. The solution can be further diluted by increasing quantity of oil or else decreasing quantity of caraway oil.

Sundry Uses

To counter insipid taste and foul smell, use caraway seeds orally. Caraway oil is also used for seasoning pickles, for flavouring cheese, breads, cakes and biscuits, as a carminative to expel and relieve flatus.

CINNAMON (Cinnamomum Zylanicum, Dalchini)

It is a small bushy tree which remains ever-green. Its dried (inner) bark and leaves are used as a comdiment or spice due to its sweet and aromatic taste, warm-effect and pleasant flavour. The inncer bark is obtained from its selective shoots, after which it is dried and treated. When fully dried, the bark curls/shrinks cylinderially or quills.

Cinnamon has high therapeutic values. Its inner bark and leaves are for flavouring curry powder, cakes and sweets, in perfumes, incense and dentifrices. The oil of cinnamon is used to flavour liquers and confectionary items, dental preparations and also pharmacy. Cinnamon oil, though quite costly, is used in flavourings and perfumes and also in the synthesis of vanillin.

Curative and Healing Properties

Digestive Disorders and Other Common Complaints

Pound and pulverise Cinnamon and boil in the water (glassful), adding a pinch of black pepper and honey—the content should be taken (a TSP) ½ an hour after each meal to allay nausea, vomiting, diarrhoea, to stimulate digestive process. If you want, you can omit black pepper and honey. But, in case of malarial fever, influenza, sore throat all the ingredients must be mixed to prevent seasonal effects of influenza. To seek relief in cold, mix honey with Cinnamon oil.

Acne and Blackheads

Mix a few drops of lime juice to paste of Cinnamon and locally apply over blackheads and pimples.

Bad Breath

Chew small pieces of Cinnamon to refresh mouth and ward off foul odour of breath.

Miscellaneous Uses

Use of cinnamon decoction/powder is highly beneficial in disorders like asthma, constipation, spasmodic afflictions, excessive bleeding and uterus perblems gonorrhoea etc. It is used as a perventive (prophylactic) measure to control surfacing of German measles. It also clears lungs and removes/expels trapped phlegm in the throat and/or lungs.

CLOVE (Syzygium Aromaticun, Laung)

Clove is commonly used in India and China to dispel bad breath from mouth and dental pain. Even now clove oil is a drug of choice for getting rid of pain in teeth. Clove is calyx-tube of the flowers of tree and when plucked, has colour, but is dried on mats. It has intoxicating fragrance has an aromatic taste, is astringent and bitter.

Therapeutic Properties

It increases blood circulation, raises heat element in blood, is aromatic, stomache, anti-pyretic, anti-flatulent, anti-phlegmatic, anti-gastric, anti-erutic, antiseptic, anaesthelic, but is carminative also.

It is rich in protein, carbohydrates, non-volatile ether extract, calcium, iron, phosphorus, potassium, niacin, thiamine, riboflavin, vitamins A and C, ash content (which is insoluble in hydrochloric acid), crude fibre. Its calorific value is 430 per 100 gms. Essential oil of cloves is derived by steam distillation of stem, leaves and buds. The resultant oil contains free eugenol, eugenol acetate and carophyllene.

Asthma, Cough

To relieve throat irritation, ease expectoration, stop cough due to pharyngitis, chew a clove with a crystal of salt. For pharyngitis and congested & sore throat, chew a burnt clove. Mix 2-4 drops of clove oil with honey and a crushed garlic clove and lick the paste in order to allay spasmodic and painful cough—either of bronchial, asthmatic or tubercular origin—but should be taken at bed time. Particularly in asthma, prepare a dicoction from six cloves and 30 ml water should be boiled, after mixing the decoction with honey, take thrice daily to induce easy expectoration.

Digestive Disorders

Cloves boost digestive functioning by promoting flow of enzymes, thereby proving their efficacy in dyspepsia and gastric irritibility. They also control vomiting, for the simple reason that they exert anaesthetic action on the gullet and stomach. To mollify all such symptoms, mix powder of fried cloves with honey and lick the same.

Cholera

Even severe symptoms of cholera can be treated by this prescription—boil 4 gms of cloves in 3 litres of water. When water has evaporated to half the quantity, sip this water (in draughts).

Whooping Cough

Take a roasted clove with honey

Ulcers

Prepare a paste of cloves and turmeric and apply over ulcers.

Teeth Care and General Dental Problems

— Apply clove oil, if there is pain but more sensitive mouths may not tolerate clove oil.
— Boil 3-4 cloves in water and garlic with it 2-3 times to get relief from tooth-ache.
— Press a clove between painful teeth or cover a clove with a cotton swab and then press in-between teeth and let out saliva.
— To strengthen gums and teeth, take a roasted clove.

Styes

Rub a clove with water on stone piece and apply over the stye, so as to eliminate painful swelling but take care the paste/ water doesn't fall into eye (s).

Influenza

Prepare a paste from ¼ TSP of ginger juice, ¼ TSP of powders of cloves and piper longum, 1 TSP of honey. It may be taken 3-4 times daily with hot water or simply licked slowly.

Hiccoughs/Hiccups

Soak 1-2 cloves in lukewarm water and take this water to have relief from bouts of hiccoughs.

Malaria

— Heat a clove in pure desi ghee and Tulsi leaf (Holy Basil) and take it in the morning to prevent Malaria.

— Prepare tea from Tulsi leaves and cloves, for being take to eliminate Malaria.

Muscular Cramps

Apply oil of clove as a poultice near/over the affected part.

Sundry Uses

Cloves are frequently used to flavour betel. For the use of spices, clove is an essential ingredient. It is also used as a flavouring agent for soaps, bath salts and perfumes.

Caution : Being an astringent and pungent, clove should not be used by persons who are suffering from sub-mucus and fibrosis/stiff jaws, also whose mouth is sensitive.

CORIANDER (Coriander Sativum, Dhania)

Coriander is used in the form of seeds and leaves in various vegetables, curries, salads, spices. its leaves contain Carbohydrates 6.3%, Protein 3.3%, Fat 0.6%, Fibre 1.2%, Moisture 86.3%. Besides, it contains iron, calcium, phosphorus, carotene, riboflavin, thiamine, niacin and vitamon-C, oxalic acid, sodium and potassium. Their calorific value per 100 gms is 44.

When ripe, coriander seeds are dried, containing an agreeable spicy taste and aromatic odour. The seeds contain Carbohydrates 21.6%, Protein 14.1%, Fat 16.1%, Minerals 4.4%, Fibre 32.6%, (per 100 gms of seeds), besides this the seeds also contain all the minerals & vitamins which have been mentioned in case of green leaves, above. Their calorific value is 288 per 100 gms.

Only seeds are used in spices but leaves are used in Chutinis, Raitas, Vegetables, Meats, Salads etc. Coriander seeds also contain fatty oil and essential oil.

Therapeutic Usage

Coriander leaves promote and strengthen various functions of stomach, thereby aiding in digestive process. They are tonic and stimulant, reduce fever, increase urinary secretion/discharge, relieve flatulence, act as an aphrodisiac, purge out phlegm/ catarrhal matter from the bronchial tubes. Coriander juice is an excellent source for compensating lassitude of vitamins A, B-1, B-2, C and iron.

Digestive Disorders

Dysentery can be treated by taking 1 TSP decoction of Dhania powder, mixing 5 mg sugar candy to it. For diarrhoea and indigestion, prepare chutni from grated coconut, dry coriander, green chillies, black grapes (without seeds) and ginger—black salt may be added to the said ingredients, if taste permits. Mix Coriander powder (60 gms), Black Pepper and black rock salt (25 gm each) —½TSP should be taken, after meals, with hot water or else coriander powder with black salt (½ TSP) will also be useful in digestive problems.

Mix 10 gms each of coriander powder, cardamom, cumin. Fry and powder all the three. A TSP, taken after meals, with skimmed curd/curd controls indigestion, diarrhoea and improves appetite. Gas-related disorders can be mollified by boiling the powdered seeds in ½ a cup of tea.

Nausea, Vomiting and Giddiness

Boil Coriander powder in water and mix sugar candy to the liquid (method, as stated earlier)

Cholesterol Rise and Renal Malfunctioning

If Coriander water is taken daily, it will reduce serum

cholesterol level and also stimulate renal functioning by its diuretic effect. Boil dry coriander seeds in water and strain the decoction after it has cooled.

Menstrual Flow (excessive)

Boil 6 gms of coriander seeds in water (½ litre) when it is reduced to half the quantity, add some sugar and take it (when it is still warm) and use for 3-4 days to get relief in excessive menstrual bleeding.

Skin Disorders

Coriander juice (1 TSP) mixed with a pinch of turmeric (Haldi) will remove blackheads, pimples and dryness of skin. But before it is applied to the face, wash your face completely. Apply this paste before retiring to bed.

Conjunctivitis

If a decoction, prepared from (freshly) dried Coriander leaves, it is used as an eye-wash, to reduce swelling and pain.

Other Uses

Volatile oil is used in medicines and for flavouring purposes. Dried Coriander is an almost inseparable ingredient of curry powder, pickles, for seasoning, sausages and confectionery, and to flavour spirits, (gin in particular).

FENUGREEK (Trigonella Foenum Graecum, Methi)

It is a commonly and frequenlty used herb, used in fresh leaves and seeds for various kitchen vegetables and medicinal uses. It is an erect, robust, annually grown herb, having strong scent. Its leaves are light green-coloured with yellow flowers and (thin) sharp (pointed) pods, but the seeds have a peculiar odour and yellow brownish appearance.

Fenugreek leaves contain 6% Carbohydrates, 4.4% Protein

0.9%, Fat 1.5%, Minerals, Fibre 1.1% and moisture 86.1% (per 100 gms of edible portion). The leaves also contain iron, calcium, phosphorus, carotene, vitamins-C, riboflavin, niacin and thiamine. Its calorific value is 49 per 100 gms.

Fenugreek seeds possess more nutritive properties and higher calories when compared to its leaves. The seeds contain Carbohydrates 44.1%, Protein 26.2%, Moisture 1.37%, Fat 5.8%, Minerals 3%, Fibre 7.2%, apart from minerals (3%) and vitamins, such as calcium, phosphorus, thiamine, niacin, riboflavin and carotene. Its calorific value, per 100 gms of edible portion, is 333.

Fenugreek seeds contain essential oil and saponin, choline and trigonelline (alkaloids). The latter exerting toxic effects on neuro-muscular medicinal preparations. Seeds, dried in air, contain some amount of nicotinic acid and trigonalline, apart from containing fixed and volatile oils, mucilage and bitter yellow colouring substance.

Healing Properties

- Serves as efficient cleansers within the body.
- Arrests excessive secretions and bleeding.
- Serves as an aphrodisaic agent.
- Increases quantity of urine and regulates secretions.
- Seeds exert soothing effect on mucus membranes, skin—by relieving skin irritation, pain and swelling.
- Used to reduce percentage of sugar content in urine and blood—for which they serve as both curative and preventive of diabetes.
- They are mucus solvents and expectorants.
- Used for backache, pain in joints, hands and feets, especially after child birth.
- Remove indigestion, flatulence, and improve liver (of slugghish liver) functioning.
- Dispel body odour and foul breath.

- Relieve sore throat, mouth ulcers and dandruff.
- Used as a douche for vaginal cleansing, in case of leucorrhoea discharge.
- Used as a beauty-aid to get rid of blackheads, pimples, wrinkles and dryness of skin.

Diabetes

Take (whole) seeds or in powder form (2 TSP) with water, or soak them in a cup of water, at night and consume the water, after mashing the seeds in the same water. A Vaidya had suggested the following prescription.

Fenugreek Powder   - 100 gms

Turmeric Powder   - 25 gms

White Pepper Powder   - 5 gms.

Take a TSP each in the morning in the morning and evening with a glass of milk (without sugar) As soon as sugar level reaches to normal levels, reduce the dose accordingly. *In certain persons, fenugreek seeds may cause high blood pressure or further cause its rise in established cases of hypertension, hence use with due caution.*

Dandruff

Highly chronic dandruff is not easy to cure but, if the disease is a consequence of some other disorder, the same can be cured. Soak 1 TSP of seeds in water and keep soaked overnight. In the morning prepare a paste using the same water and apply over scalp, and let the paste remain for ½ hour whereafter the paste should be washed off with Shikakai/soapnut (Reetha) solution. Alternatively, apply paste of fresh leaves of fenugreek and apply over scalp before you take bath.

Fever and Respiratory Disorders

When moistened with water, fenugreek seeds soften which should be used while making tea—it is an almost alternative to quinine and can melt sticky substances also. The tea, so

150

prepared, is also useful in initial disorders of respiratory passage. It also shortens incubation period and dispels suspected pneumonia, sinusitis, catarrh, bronchitis and influenza. Fenugreek tea also induces body perspiration and expels toxic elements. If a few drops of lemon juice are added to the beverage, it will hasten effect and add to flavour also. To dervie even still quicker results, keep on complete fast.

Stomach and Digestive Disorders

Fenugreek tea is a great cleanser—it ably cleanses bowels, intestines, stomache, kidneys (rather whole urinary tract) and organs of respiration. As the mild coating, provided by fenugreek, a protective layer is formed, as a result of which it is useful in ulcers also.

Body Odour and Foul Breath

These conditions emanate from the body, simply due to deposit of toxins or/and mucus in gastro-intestinal tract, nasal cavities, vaginal passage, blood stream, other oral passages which conditions can be removed by using fenugreek tea as a mouth-wash (which can penetrate far deeper into the said body parts).

The volatile oils of fenugreek are still far more powerful and effective, as they have the capacity to penetrate deep into cell tissues and sweat glands, thereby removing general indolency and affections (of various etiologies). In a way whole body is rejuvenated.

Sundry Uses

- To retain vitamins/minerals always steam-boil the leaves.
- Prepare a sweetdish (Halwa) like this : Fry finely powdered seeds in pure desi ghee, mix wheat flour and sugar to it—it should be taken 2-3 times (say a TBSP or so) with milk to have normal delivery.

- If gruel of seeds is given to a nursing mother, it will increase milk-flow.

- Fenugreek seeds are used as a condiment for flavouring vegetables, in curries, curry powder, bread, bakery, cheese, cosmetics and hair tonics, in medicinal preparations, preparing soups and stews, and spice blends.

PARSLEY (Petroselinum Crispum, Prajmoda)

Parsley is available in plain and curled leaves which are shiny and green leaves that originate from a short stem. In addition, herb has a fleshy and aromatic tap root. It is a store house of vitamins A & C.

Parsley is comprised of carbohydrates 13.5%, Protien 5.9%, Fat1%, Minerals 3.2%, Fibre 1.8%, Moisture 74.6% (per 100 gms of edible portion). As for minerals and vitamins, it contains iron, calcium, phosphorus, carotene, riboflavin, niacin, thiamine, and vitamin-C. Its calorific value being 87 (per 100 gms). Its fruits contain coumarin, and essential oil contains Apoil, apart from these two ingredients, it also contains glucoside Apiin.

Therapeutic Uses

It is an excellent blood purifier due to its rich content of Ascorbic acid (vitamin-C). It increases secretion of urine, relieves flatulence. It also increases functioning of thyroid and adrenal glands, and restores them to their normal functionality levels. Parsley is highly effective in high blood pressure, menstrual, disgestive, genito-urinary, Eye disorders. Wounds, insect-biles, boils, and bad breath are also cured. Parsley is an uncommon herbal variety which is rarely/sparsely grown in India, hence its use is not common.

Precaution : Whether juice is taken independently or mixed with other juices, its total quantity must not exeed 60 ml.

Digestive Disorders

To prevent gas formation in intestines and stomach, improve digestion, take springs of fresh herb (1 TSP), or else take a ¼ TSP of dried powder of its herb with water. If fresh parsley is tough, it needs to be masticated properly.

High Blood Pressure

Parsely has the property to keep blood vessels (especially the arteries and capillaries) in healthy state, thus maintaining their flexibility. To overcome problem of high blood pressure, simmer it in water and consume it in the form of a beverage which may be taken 5-6 times in a day. The dosage and frequency can be graduated and moderated in view of rise/fall of blood pressure.

Genito-Urinary Problems

It removes calculii from kidneys, bladder, ureters, is also useful in conditions like Nephritis, albuminuria, cystitis etc. It can be taken in juice or powder form, as indicated above. It can also be used in dropsy.

Eye Disorders

To improve eye-sight and ailments connected with optic nerve, in cases of corneal ulceration, ophthalmia, cataract, sluggishness of pupils, conjunctivitis, mix parsley juice with carrot juice.

Mesntrual Irregularities

To build up and improve general health of ladies, to restore normal menstrual flow (in case of retarded or scanty menses) and to regulate menstrual periods, to relieve cramps, use parsely juice which, preferably, should be mixed wtih carrot, cucumber and beet juices.

Wounds, Boils and Insect Bites

Locally apply bruised parsley on sites where there are signs of bites and stings. It may also be applied over inflamed/bruised joints. It will induce expulsion of pus where suppuration has set in or is about to take place. Steep and oil it in water till it becomes juicy and soft—the resultant pulp may be applied over boils (when it is still bearably hot) wrapped and with some piece of cloth.

Bad/Foul odour From mouth

Roughly chopped springs should be boiled in water (quantity 2 cups), adding 3-4 cloves or powder to it, and frequently stirred, during boiling process or when it is about to cool. Then strain the contents which may be used, as a gargle and/or mouthwashs, 3-4 times a day.

Miscellaneous Uses

Parsley can be cooked with root or green vegetables (like cabbage) or freely used in soups, salads. After drying, it should be preserved in a bottle/Tin. It can also be added to juices of beets, carrots, spinach, lattuce, celery and other raw vegetables. Gently simmer parsley for 10-15 minutes, and use it as an effective beverage.

RAUWOLFIA (Rauwolfia Serpentina, Sarapaganda) ·

To begin with, 'Ciba' was, perhaps, the first allopathic pharmaceutical company that introduced 'Serpentina Tablet' into the market to control high blood pressure. Its nomeclation is attributed to Dr. Leonard Rauwolfia, a German physician and botanist. The herb is erect, having a smooth stem. A legendary Ayurvedic authority, charak, in his monumental treatise (charak sanhita) recommended its use. For medicinal purposes, bark and dried roots are utilised.

Therapeutic Uses

Fairly large use of this herb is attributed to its roots having

154

two important alkaloids (viz Serpentine and Ajmaline). Its roots contain fairly large amounts of total alkaloids, apart from containing plenty of starch and resin which, when incinerated, leave back residual ash that consists of manganese traces of iron, silicate, phosphate, pot. carbonate.

It cures insanity, lowers blood pressure, removes insomnia, dispels hysterical fits and also urticaria. It also reduces/lowers blood pressure and fever. It is also claimed, though not verified and confirmed, that it facilitates expulsion of the foetus by stimulating contraction of the uterus.

Insomnia And High Blood Pressure

Since the herb has higher properties of inducing sleep, *it must not be used in case of infants* and children to quieten them, by inducing sleep by the use of this herb or if a patient is having gout or phlegm or has tendency to develop such symptoms, in acute cases of insomnia, due to whichever etiology (cause). Powder of herb's root should be given in 0.50 to 1.25 gms with some scented vehicle (say aqua of rose/sandal). As it is non-stimulative, a dose 0.25 gms can be given to the sufferer at bedtime, to induce sound sleep, while the chronic patients may have a dose each in the morning and evening/at night before retiring to bed.

As for high blood pressure ½ TSP of powder of its root can be taken, thrice daily to quell ouslaught of hypertension.

Let it be noted that if insomnia be the cause of hypertension, a sound sleep at night will help in lowering blood pressure, as both the disorders cannot be segregated from each other — if you have high blood pressure you are, most likely, not going to have sleep (much less a sound sleep) and if you are unable to enjoy a sound sleep you will, mostly likely, find your blood pressure raised.

Hysteria

Let me dispel a myth—both men and woman, can suffer

155

from hysterical disorders, though women are more prone to this disorder. To say that only women suffer from this disorder is a total negation of truth, whereas the fact of the matter being that both sexes are equally vulnerable. Give one gram of powdered root, with milk, thrice daily, but continue the treatment until full recovery is obtained.

Insanity

Melancholic, sad, depressed, weak and lean persons easily derive benefit from this herb whereas those with robust and sturdy constitution and who are extremely irritatble cannot derive any benefit. But, in all the cases of insanity, the patient's B. P. should be measured. If B. P. is high, then the drug can be used, but *it is unsuitable for persons having Low B. P.*—the reason being that the herb lowers B. P. and if given in low B. P., it will further lower the B.P. Give 1 gm powder of the root with goat's mik (200/225 ml), adding sugar/sugar-candy, if desired.

Hives/Urticaria Nettle Rash

Give one gram powder of the root with water to get relief from urticarial itching.

Rauwolfia is used for medicinal purposes only and is, thus, not used for any other purpose. In any case, do not exceed the indicated dose/frequency.

WINTER CHERRY (Withenia Somnifera, Ashwatgandha)

It is a middle/small sized, erect shrub and its stems & branches have star-shaped minute hair. Its leaves are egg-shaped, having pale, green flowers in clusters. It has yellow seeds and red fruits.

For various medicinal purposes, it has somniferine, an alkaloid, indefinite amorphous substances, sugar-found in the water soluble portion of its root extract which also consists of a black resin that contains, apart from other properties, mixture of fatty acids, besides glucose, some alkaloids, pot. nitrate and tannin.

Curative Properties

- Induces sleep and sedates agitated nerves
- Induces sound, undistrubed and deep sleep.
- Treats various conditions of cough and cold.
- Treats tuberuculosis, scrofula.
- Removes non-specific/general debility.
- Corrects disordered digestion, improves nutrition and increases appetite.
- Useful in rheumatic and artheritic disorders like pain, swelling etc.
- Cures female sterility.
- Has antibacterial and antibiotic properties.
- Used extensively for various skin infections, such as wounds, bed-sores, syphilitic sores, carbuncles ulcers etc.
- Used also to enhance libido and sexual vitality in males, to treat spermatorrhoea, premature ejaculation.
- Used as a fomentation to sore eyes.

Pregnant ladies must not use it, as the drug has the capacity to abort foetus but, in normal conditions, they can also use it.

Arthritis & Rheumatism : An experienced lady doctor bad advocated use of following prescription for arthritis.

Powder of winter cherry	-	100 gms
Almond	-	50 gms
Aniseed	-	50 gms
Sugar Candy	-	100 gms

Pulverise almond, aniseed and sugar candy (to be mixed last of all) separately, mix all the contents alongwith powder

157

of winter cherry. Take a TSP (heaped) in the morning and evening with hot milk. Diabetics should not use sugar candy. The treatment has to be continued for a fairly long period. Those who are prone to cold, should replace aniseed with dry ginger powder. For rheumatism ½ TSP should be taken twice daily with water but, first try the first formulation.

Insomnia

Take ½-1 TSP with of powder of its root with hot milk at night. Since the herb possesses high amount of narcotic effect, it can quickly induce sleep.

General Debility

Take 2 gm dose, (thrice daily with water) of powder of winter cherry's root to treat general debility.

Tuberculosis, Cough and Cold

Prepare decoction of its roots, adding honey and long pepper to the decoction which is also very beneficial in treating tuberculosis of lymph glands (especially appearing in the neck).

Take 2 ½-3 gms powder or decoction of root to quell even serious attaks of cold and cough. But, in case of chest complaints, berries should be used.

Aphrodisiac Uses

To enhance sexual urge/competence (libido), take 2-4 gms of powdered root with ghee/milk, as per convenience. Such a dose (2-3times daily) will also prove beneficial in case of involuntary ejacuation/spermatorrhoea. To hasten quicker effect for curing the said conditions, take the said dose by mixing it with unequal quantities of honey & ghee, long pepper.

Digestive Disorders

Winter cherry is very beneficial to normalise and restore nutritional process, including dyspepsia and loss of appetite (Anorexia).

Skin Disorders

For boils, swelled feet and hands, apply fomentation of leaves of the plant. But paste of leaves should be applied to kill lice. In case of Syphilitic sores/boils and cerbuncles, prepare an ointment by boiling its leaves in any fatty vehicle, like ghee, and apply to wound and bed-sores. For local application over ulcers, swellings and carbuncles, it is better to apply a paste, processed from roots and leaves.

Eye infection.

To get relief in sore eyes, apply fomentation from winter cherry's leaves.

VASAKA (Adhatoda Vasika, Adoosa)

There is an oft-repeated addage that cough, cold, sore throat and phlegm cannot exist where there is Vasaka which is used in various cough mixtures in allopathic syrups and linctuses, in ayurvedic and Unani Medicines. It is called the Malabear Nut tree, having evergreen shrub. It has four-seeded and capsular fruits, lance-shaped and large leaves, having white or purple flowers. Vasaka leaves contain an essential oil and vaseline (an alkaloid). Roots, leaves and flowers of Vasaka have been used as an effective device for relieving cold, cough, bronchitis and tuberculosis, apart from asthma, when its dried leaves are to be smoked.

Cough, Asthma & Bronchitis, Tuberculosis

Prepare 'Gulkand' from fresh flower-petals of Vasaka, adding some sugar crystal, after which it should be rinsed and kept in a jar of glass/china clay, and should be stirred in the morning and evening. A TSP should be taken with cow' milk in the morning and at night, before retiring to bed.

In order to liquify sputum, for easy expectoration and relieving irritating cough, 25 ml juice of vasaka leaves may be taken 3 times daily with honey. U. C. Dutt had rightly declared that "no man, suffering from pthisis, need dispair as long as vasaka plant exists."

Boil and strain seven plant leaves and mix with 21 gms of honey. It (decoction) will provide relief in coughs, or eat 12 gm vasaka leaves twice daily (It should be processed from 180 gms of jaggery and 60 gms of flowers. Smoke dried leaves, in the same manner, as beedi/cigarette is smoked.

Diarrhoea, Dysentery and Intestinal Worms

Prepare a decoction of 30 gm bark and root, and take 25 gms 2-3 times for 3 cosecutive days or else take a TSP dose (thrice daily) of juice of vasaka leaves to cause expulsion of worms from intestines. Its juice, in 2-4 gm doses, will prove effective in disorders of dysentery & diarrhoea.

Skin Disorders

Apply poultice of its seeds over wounds of recent origin, in inflammatory swellings and rheumatic joints and other manifestations. Prepare a warm decoction of its leaves in various skin diseases, including scabies.

General information : For decoction, use dried or fresh vasaka leaves and the resultant decocted liquid should be mixed with honey and juice of ginger—usual dose being 3 to 6 TSP, or else reduce the dried Vasaka Leaves (either for processing decoction using it as powder), normally a gm dose would suffice. Both powder and decoction are used while preparing cough syrups to mollify infections of respiratory passage. If powder of its bark root is used, its dose will vary from 1-2 grams, but when bark is used for decoction, its doses would vary from 5 to 10 TSP, of course, in divided doses, spread over 2-4 doses per 24 hours.

TURMERIC (Curcuma Longa, Haldi, Haridra)

Turmeric is an essential ingredient of various kitchen

160

preparations and used as spice, and for its therapeutic utility it is almost an indispensible item. Application of turmeric poultice has been in vogue for healing wounds of both human beings and animals. Its plant resembles a ginger plant, and smell of its leaves is fairly sweet, frangrant-akin to mango pollen. Its fresh root is dried in the sun. It is a food preservative, a favourite and useful condiment-used in vegetarian & non-vegetarian preparations. Now-a-days it is used for skin and beauty care to improve complexion and divests the body from nauseating odour. Obtan of Haldi is an age old device, used at the time of marriage (prior to) for both bride and her groom. But, Haldi should not be used, orally or locally, in excess, as it has its own reactions.

Curative and Healing Properties.

- It is sour and stringent
- Is a tonic, blood purifier and promotes action of stomach.
- The Rhizome of turmeric is stimulant, aromatic and tonic
- It is a skin tonic, provides natural gloss and royal lustre and glow, imparts youthful vitality and vigour.
- It is diuretic, expectorant, wound-healer, expectorant, aromatic, analgesic, germincidal, antiflatulent, anti-billious, anti-inflammatory, bone-setter and protector of eyes and eye vision.
- Corrects disorders relating to digestion.
- Restores normal functioning of system
- Raises R. B. Cs and purifies impure blood

100 gms of edible portion of turmeric contains carbohydrates 69.4%, Protein 6.3%, Fat 5.1%, Fibre 2.6%. As for vitamins & minerals it contains iron, calcium, phorphorus, thiamine, niacin and carotene. It calorific value (per 100 gms) is 349.

Anaemia

Mix juice of raw turmeric with honey and take it daily. It will raise R. B. Cs in the blood, due to its rich content of iron.

Asthma, Bronchial Asthma, Cough and Cold

Take a TSP of turmeric powder and mix with a glassful of hot milk which should, preferably, be taken on empty stomach or else taken even 2-3 times. It will also cure bronchial asthma. It will also soothe throat irritation and chronic cough. To have still quicker and better results mix ½ TSP of fresh turmeric powder with 50-40 ml. milk. To stop running from nose, due to cold, inhale smoke of burnt piece of turmeric.

If infants and children are suffering from cold, mix turmeric with caraway or seeds cumin (1 TSP and ¼ TSP respectively) and add to boil (letting of cool). The decoction should be sweetened with honey and given in dose of 30 ml.

Worms (Intestinal) and Intestinal Disorders

To expel intestinal worms, mix a pinch of salt to juice (20 ml) of raw turmeric, and taken daily early in the mornings for a few days. In case of chronic diarrhoea, take dry powder or rhizome (underground stems) juice, mixed with water or butter/milk which also is a preventive of flatulence and a useful antiseptic.

Boils and Sprains

To hasten healing process, apply turmeric powder to boils or roast roots of dried turmeric and then reduce to ashes which should be dissolved in a cup of water and then applied over the boils—it will also ripen, mature and burst the boils and throw out the oozing substances. Apply a paste, prepared from turmeric powder and lime, and apply over sprained parts or swellings triggered by sprains.

Beauty and Skin Care

Prepare an ubtan (paste) from turmeric powder, sandalwood powder, coconut/mustard oil and apply over face, hands arms, neck, feet etc. when the paste has dried, same may be removed and washed off with lukewarm or fresh tepid water. It will impart glow to the body parts, improve complexion, remove blemishes, acne and spots, but the paste has to be applied for some time continuously, to obtain better results.

ASHOKA (Saraca Indica, Ashoka)

It is a small, evergreen tree, having a smooth brown-coloured bark and compound leaves. Bark of Ashoka tree is used generally for medicinal purposes. Its bark contains catechol and tanmine but the powdered ash of Ashoka bark contains sodium, potassium, phosphate, iron, silica, calcium, magnesium, aluminum and strontium. Apart from that, a crystalline glycosidal substance (with galactose as the constituent sugar) has also been isolated from Ashoka bark.

Ashoka bark is used extensively in Ayurveda for containing bleeding/secretion from the uterus, hence its use in the form of a tonic for the uterus. It is said to exert salutary and curative effect on the mucus membranes that lines the uterus and on ovarian tissues.

Menstrual Problems

Decoction of bark of tree contains and makes up for the blood lost during menstruation or due to the presence of fibroids in the uterus. It also modifies and corrects leucorrhoeal discharge and is an efficient substitute for ergot, administered to ladies in mesntrual bleeding. Boil 60 gms of bark in 20 ml of milk and 240 ml of water, when the quantity reduces to 60 ml, it should be allowed to boil. Start taking it from 4th day of menstruation and continue till bleeding gets under control, but decoction should be prepared afresh daily. Consult some Vaidya about dosage and its freqnecy alongwith other safeguards and guidance. The resultant decocted liquid should be divided into two or three doses per day, or modified according to situation.

Dysentery

Use fluid extract (15-60 drops per dose) of Ashoka flowers to get relief in bleeding piles or else use the decoction of bark. Grind the flowers to yield the fluid extract.

Piles

Prepare a decoction, as indicated under menstrual problems heretofore.

Diabetes

Dried flowers of Ashoka are said to be beneficial in diabetes also.

INDIAN ALOE (Aloe Barbadensis, Ghrita Kumari, MUsabbar, Ghee Kanwar)

Aloe is used in Homoeopathy also for various alimentary disorders and is used as a vegetable (Pulp only) and in medicines. Indian aloe is an erect plant, having pale-green, smooth, fleshy leaves, lapeting to a blunt point, having horny prickles at the margins. Its flowers are either orange coloured or yellow and cylindrical (in shape). For processing medicines, juice of fleshy leaves is utilised.

The leaves of aloe restore disordered nutrition to normalcy, contain bleeding and enhance libido and regulate menstrual period.

Liver and Digestion related disorders intestinal worms

Aloe herb is beneficial in spleen and liver disorders, as it stimulates and regualtes functioning thereof. In addition, it is also useful in enlargement of liver, spleen. To treat such disorders, administer pulp of a leaf with ginger and black salt, for ten days or so. The leaves promote digestion, improve function of stomach. Its leaves should be used, in the form of salad, to get rid of flatulence, constipation, indigestion. Further, its leave posess the property to kill and expel intestinal worms for which boil the leaves in water and administer the condensed juice of leaves, but it would be better if guidance of a Vaidya is sought before use.

Skin Disorders

Apply fresh juice of aloe leaves locally to treat painful and inflamed parts of the body, but do not use in around or over the eyes.

Rheumatism

If you want to get rid of rheumatism, sciatica and lumbago, take daily pulp of one leaf. It will have also a soothing and salutary effect.

LEMON BALM (Mellisa Officinalis, Bililotan)

The plant belongs to the mint family which has egg-shaped leaves and small pale, white or pink flowers, has an amiable odour, though strong, that is akin to lemon. Its flowering tops and leaves are utilised in drugs.

Drinking tea of lemon balm is said to prolong longevity, strengthen brain and nervous system—in general it renews youthful vigour, prevents alopecia (baldness) and relieves languishing temperament/nature. Apart from all the said properties, it improves and promotes function of the stomach. The herb has also antipyretic properties, removes bad taste from the mouth, strengthens the gums, dispels ill-effects of poisonous bites of insects. Its leaves are said to be beneficial in cardiac and hepatic disorders.

Nerve tonic and sedative

Put 25-30 gms of herb in a ½ litre of water and let the same remain there for 12 hours, after which time strain the infusion and consume, by and by, in small doses, within a day. It will sharpen memory, revive spirits, keep mood upbeat, counteract depression, have sedative and tranquilising impact on nervous system and also prevent brain fatigue.

Fevers

Tea prepared from its leaves will lower body's temperature.

Further, its leaves and stems are also used for treating various heart and liver disorders, especially those which are directly related to nervous origin.

Cut and dry the plants under shade, when those are in full bloom, so as to retain and preserve natural colour.

13

List of Diseases Cured/ Treated by Various Herbs & Referral Books

VARIOUS HERBS & REFERRAL BOOKS

Note : Due to space crunch, only most commonly used and well known herbs have been described heretofore. But it must not be construed that herbs, which have not been dealt with in this book, are not important or they do not possess any therapeutic and healing properties. Truly speaking, it was not physically possible to describe each and every herb within the ambit of this book hence the readers, who are curious to know more about the herbs, should refer to relevant and standard books; some of which are listed hereunder.

1. **'Herbs For All Seasons'** by Homphill Rosemary

2. 'Herbs That Heal' by H. K. Bakhru
3. 'Medicinal Herbs' by Penelop ody.
4. 'Glossary of Indian Medicinal Plants' by R. N. Chopra, I. C. Chopra and S. H. Nayar
5. 'Herbal Teas For Health and Healing' by Mabey Richard
6. 'Herbal Remedies' By N. N. Saha
7. 'Herbal Foods' by N. Ramaswamy Pillai
8. 'Miracles of Indian Herbs' by Ganpati Singh Verma
9. 'Ayurvedic Cure For Common Diseases' by Murthy and Pandey
10. 'Drug Plants of India' by V. S. Agarwal, B. Ghosh
11. 'Spices and condiments' by J. S. Pruthi
12. 'Medicial Plants of India And Pakistan' by J. F. Dastoor
13. 'The Magic of Herbs in Daily Living' by Lucus Richard
14. 'Medicinal Plants of India' by G. V. Satyawati and Ashok K. Gupta
15. 'Herbal Remedies & Home Comforts' by Jill Nice.
16. 'Foods that Heal' by H. K. Bakhru.
17. 'Medicinal Herbs & Essential Oil' by A. Gardiner.
18. 'The Bael Cultivation And Processing' by R. N. Singh and Sushant. K. Roy.
19. 'Nutritive Values of Indian Foods' by Gopalan and Balasubramanian.
20. 'The Complete New Herbal Elm Tree Books' by Mabey Richard, Madiyntre Michael, Michael Pamela and Stevers John.
21. 'The Complete Book of Home Remedies' by Abdul Hameed Saheb H.
22. 'Be You Own Doctor' by Dr. Kanta Gupta

23. 'Food For Good Health' by Dr. S. K. Sharma

24. 'Juice Therapy' by Dr. S. K. Sharma

25. Ayurvedic Cure For Common Diseases by Acharya Vipul Rao.

26. 'Natural Home Remedies' by H. K. Bakhru

LIST OF DISORDERS AND REMEDIES

Anaemia

Ash Gourd

Celery Blood Wort
Chicory
Dill
Fenugreek
Gokulkanta
Hog Weed
Onion,
Wormwood

Asthma & Bronchitis

Aniseed
Arjuna
Asafoatida
Bay Berry
Bishop's weed
Calamees
Celery
C. Myroblan
Chicory
Clove
Dhatur/Datura
Euphorbia

Arthritis & Rheumatism

Alfalfa
Aloe (Indian Aloe)

Castor Seeds/Oil
Celery
Chirayata
Colchicum
Garlic
Gokulkanta
Indian Gooseberry
Indian Sarasaparilla

Arthritis & Rheumatism

Castor seeds
Indian Senna
Indian Squill
Ispaghula/Isobgole
Leadwort
Lemon grass
Meduca
Nut meg
Pepper (Black)
Rosemary
Saffron
Sage
Turpeth

Garlic
Ginger
Hogweed
Holy Basil (Tulsi)
Hyssop
Indian Acalypha
Indian Gooseberry
Indian Squill
Kantakari
L. inseed
Marjoram
Rhubarb
Turmeric
Vasaka
Cataract
Aniseed
Fenugreek
Garlic Winter Cherry
Indian sorrel
Indian Mallow
Parsley
Catarrh
Aniseed
Garlic,
Cataract
Aniseed
Fenugreek
Garlic
Indian Mallow
Parsley
Abdominal Pains, Colic & Peritonitis
Bishop's weed
Better chamomile

Vasaka
Winter cherry
Boils, Burns & Scalds
Betel leaves
Butea
Chalmongra
Chebulic Myroblan
Cumin seeds
Curry leaves
Dill
Indian Mallow
Margosa
Marigold
Parsley
Potato
Tamarind
Turmeric

Zigyphus

Constipation
Bishop's weed
Parslane
Cassia
Chicory
Fennel
Hog weed
Indian Aloe
Indian Senna
Isapghula
Snake Gourd
Tamarind
Bael Fruit

170

Blood wort
Cassia,
Corriander
Cumin seeds
Dill
Ginger
Garlic,
Asafoetida
Hog weed
Indian Spikenand
Isapghula
Marjoram

Cholera
Fenugreek
Cloves
Lemon Grass
Lemon
Mint leaves
Aniseed
Onion,

Betel leaves
Butea
Cardamom
Clove
Fenugreek
Garlic
Ginger
Holy Basil
Linseed
Liquorice
Pepper
Sage
Turmeric

Belleric Myroblan
Linseed
Liquorice.
Rhubarb

Common Cold
Bishop's weed
Cassia
Cinnamon
Cumin seeds
Ginger
Holy Basil
Hyssop
Nutmeg
Onion
Pepper
Liquorice
Vasaka

Cough & Sore Throat
Bay Berry
Belleric Myroblan
Coriander
Chebulic Myroblan
Chicory
Cumin seeds
Curry Leaves
Mint leaves
Holy Basil
Isapghula
Indian Gooseberry
Indian Pennywort

Diphtheria
Garlic
Dropsy
Alfalfa

Vasaka
Diabetes
Butea
Curry leaves
Fenugreek
Jambul Fruit
Bael leaves & fruit
Indian Gooseberry
Medhuca
Tenner's Cassia
Dysentery & Diarrhoea

Arjuna
Bael Fruit
Banyan
Belleric Myroblan
Black Nightshade
Bishop's Weed
Butea
Ash gourd
Curry leaves
Fenugreek
Indian Hemp
Rosemary
Sage
Trailing Eclipta
Dengue Fever & Fever
Blood wort
Casia
Chirayata
Coriander
Dhatura (Datura)
Devil's Tree
Fenugreek

Arjuna
Belleric Myroblan
Digitalis
Euphorbia
Gokulkanta
Kantakari
Marjoram
Dysuria
Kantakari
Parslane
Sandalwood
Eczema
Babool (Keekar)
Butea
Linseed
Madhuca
Dandruff & falling of Hair
Alfalfa
Gout
Castor seeds
Celery
Gokulkanta
Holy Basil
Turpeth
Zizyphus
Glycosuria
Ashoka
Bay Berry
Butea
Calamus
Chirayata
Isapghula
Indian Berberry

Garlic, Hermal
Hog weed
Holy Basil
Indian Bay Berry
Indian Mallow
Indian Sorrel
Lemon Balm
Lamon Grass
Saffron
Sandalwood
Snake Gourd
Tenner's casia

Gall Stones
Celery
Kantakart
Glaucoma
Indian Gooseberry

Heart Problems
Alfalfa
Arjuna
Blood Wort
Digitalis
Garlic
Hog weed
Indian Gooseberry
Kantakari
Lemon Balm
Onion
Peepal (Pipal)
Snake Gourd

Herpes
Linseed
High Blood Pressure
Alfalfa

Indian Sarasaparilla
Lead wort
Nut meg
Parslane
Poppy seeds
Sandal wood
Vasaka
Wood Apple

Migraine & Headache
Bishop's weed
Betel leaves
Cardamon
Cinnamon
Clove
Ginger
Henna
Indian Hemp
Bitter Chamomile
Blood wort
Calamus
Caraway seeds
Cardamom
Casia
Celery
Cheublic Myroblan
Cinnamon
Clove
Coriander
Cumin seeds
Curry leaves
Dill
Fennel
Asafoetida
Fenugreek

Arjuna
Bloodwort
Garlic
Jaudice Berry
Parsley
Rauwolfia
Hysteria
Asafoetida
Ash Gourd
Picrorhiza
Saffron
Trumeric
Acidity/Dyspepsia/
Flatulence/Indigestion
Aniseed
Belleric Myroblan
Influenza
Fenugreek
Holy Basil
Marjoram
Onion
Saffron
Cardamom
Insomnia (Sleeplessness)
Aniseed
Celery
Cumin seeds
Indian Hemp
Indian Sorrel
Nutmeg
Brahmi
Jatamanshi
Poppy seeds
Rauwolfia

Ginger
Hyssop
Indian Aloe
Mint leaves
Indian Sarasaparilla
Indian Spakenard
Lemon Blam
Marjoram
Margosa/Neem
Pepper
Rosemary
Saffron
Onion
Garlic
Tamerind
Turmeric
Low Blood Pressure
Rauwolfia
Indian Spikenard
Lumbago/Low back pain
Betel leaves
Garlic
Indian Aloe
Lemon Grass
Cirrhosis of liver and
Other problems of liver
Chicory
Dandelion
Garlic
Henna
Hog weed
Indian Aloe
Jaundiac Berry
Kantakari

174

Valerian
Jaundice
Chicory
Gokulkanta
Hog weed
Indian Aloe
Indian Pennywort
Jaudice Berry
Snake Gourd
Kidney Stones
Celery
Holy Basil
Leucoderma
Garlic
Holi Basil
Leadwort
Menstrual Disorder
Ashoka
Asafoetida
Bamboo
Blood wort
Chicory
Dill
Ginger
Henna
Hermal
Indian Hemp
Indian Spikanard
Indian Squill
Jaudice Berry
Lemon grass
Pergularia
Tenner's Cassia
Nausea

Lemon Balm
Snake Gourd
Measles
Cinnamon
Turmeric
Muscular Cramps
Clove
Ginger
Kantakari
Liquorice
Pepper
Myopia
Luquorice
Orchitis
Madhuca

Cinnamon
Coriander
Fenugreek
Sandalwood
Turmeric
Lemon
Pleurisy
Celery
Hogweed
Linseed
Prickly Heat
Sandalwood
Prosiasis
Black Nightshade
Pyorrhoea
Holy Basil
Pepper

Cassia
Curry leaves
Hog weed
Nephritis
Linseed
Parsley
Orchitis
Madhuca
Peptic Ulcer
Ash Gourd
Bael Fruit
Pharyngitis
Cardamom
Acne/Pimples
Arjuna
Sinusitis
Ephedra
Fenugreek
Scurvy
Jaudice
Wood Berry
Sptrain
Hyssop
Marjoram
Turmeric
Sphillis
Gokulkanta
Indian Marrow
Indian Pennywort
Poppy seeds
Tonsillitis
Babul (Keekar)
Kantakari
Madhuca

Dhobi's Itch/Ringworm
Butea
Cassia
Corriander
Cumin seeds
Holy Basil
Hysop
Indian squill
Leadwort
Lemon Grass
Turmeric
Sciatica
Bitter Chamomile
Indian Aloe
Nutmeg
Celery
Chalmogra
Ginger
Indian Hemp
Linseed
Marigold
Onion
Water Cherry
Typhoid
Jaudice Berry
Ulcers
Bamboo
Fenugreek
Hog weed
Leadwort
Vaginitis
Chebulic Myroblan
Isapghula
Whooping Cough

176

Teeth disorders and toothache

Asafoetida
Babul
Banyan
Clove
East Indian
Rosemary
Holy Basil
Indian Mallow
Marjoram
Onion
Pepper

Tuberculosis

Ash Gourd

Dhatura/Datura
(Use with utmost care)
Garlic

Note : *Under one heading (of disease) many herbs have been mentioned, but it is not that each patient will react positively to all of them. It is a simple method of pick and choose, error—and-trial. Some herbs may even react instantly, hence care should always be taken while using any herb. Better still, seek proper guidance from a herbalist or an ayurvedic physician, leaving nothing to chance.*

BABY CARE
PREVENTIVE AND CURATIVE TREATMENT FOR VARIOUS COMMON DISORDERS

Infants & Children Diseases

It is necessary to point out that the effects of tension, stress, worry and anxiety, dietary indiscretions, like consuming wind-creating foods, spicy and condimented food, irregular food timings of mothers are sufficient reasons for transmitting the fall-out symptoms to her off-spring, escepally to the breast-fed infants.

Infantile Colic

1. Boil ¼ TSP Fennal Seeds in some quantity of milk for 5-10 minutes, and then strain the liquid. Give in doses of ¼-1 TSP, in divided doses, according to age.

2. Gripe Water 1 TSP-2 TSP or even more may be given to the babies. The mothers should also take a TBSP simultaneously for the simple reason that they will pass on the resultant benefits to their babies through the milk they feed (breast milk) to their babies.

3. Mix Caraway Seeds, Fennel or Dill Seeds to one cup of boiling water which should be allowed to stand for 15-20 minutes and then, strained by means of a fine fitter. Give 1 TSP after every 2-4 hours, depending on symptoms and also the relief attained.

4. Slice one Carrot with a small piece of Fennel and gently cook in water. When it has softened, strain the same and serve it, after mixing honey with it to babies who are served solid foods also.

5. Prepare a weak (mild) tea either from Catmint or Chammomile (1TSP) in a cup of boiling water and infuse the same and, then finely filter. Add some honey to make it more palatable.

6. If no other herb is available, simple give a TSP of boiled water after it has been luke-warmed.

Nappy Rash

This is not a disease but simply an indicator to low grade hygienic upkeep. Do not wash baby's nappy in a detergent/soap mixed water. If you use such deodorising devices, make sure you have fully rinsed all soapy water. The infection can surface on and around thighs, buttocks, genitals, thigh folds. After defecation/urination wash the parts with very light boric acid lotion and then apply some non-irritant cream, cream of vitamin E or a wax barrier cream (neutral white). But avoid using any synthetic Panties or Nappies. Leave the bottom open and bare for sometime, changing the undersheets as frequently as possible, especially when wet/soiled. while washing the Nappies add a few drops of dettol or savlon lotion.

If, despite-all the usual precautions, the baby still has rashes, change your diet to a bland one. Do not use highly seasoned, fried, fatty and acidic foods, spices.

Crying/Weeping Babies

Some babies continue to cry unless and until they are carried in arms, some cry due to some disorder or distress, some might been stung by some insect, while others may be crying for feed of milk. It is height of indiscreet imprudence to ascribe every cry of a baby to hunger. In 90 out of 100 cases, the cause lies elsewhere. If you resort to breast-feed the child, in your eagerness to quieten him, you are simply ignoring your duty. If it is colic, use anyone of the devices given under. Infantile colic, or if wetted nappy/bed sheet be the cause, change the same, and apply some baby powder or cream.

Always add some sweatener, like sugar/honey, to baby's drink when given orally.

Chicken Pox

Chicken pox is not common in childhood and almost all children experience this agonising disorder. If the disease dose not affect mouth and eyes, it is not a serious manifestation. Chicken pox can be inferred when there is feverish shiver, water runs from nose, there is nausea, pain and ache which, in fact, are the initial symptoms that alarm about impending onset of this malady. After a gap of 3-4 days the patient develops patches of (flat) red spots that develop into blisters and, then, break- later on crusts develop over them and that's the time, when there is itching and, will leave scars, if not topped and dangerously spread. Innocent children cannot resist the impulse to scratch and itch. If itching is uncontrollable, then their hands should be tied but protect the eyes and mouth, using suitable eye-baths or mouth-washes mentioned earlier in this book.

No medicine is generally called for but consult a physician if the infection permeates to mouth and eyes. Wash the spots gently and softly with witch hazel water but, if it is irritating, a piece of cloth may be dipped in a diluted & weak water, wrung and then applied over the spots, or else add cider vinegar (½ cup) to water (for bathing).

Crush fresh garden peas and the boil liquid may be applied to erupted spots which will remove irritation and soothe the skin. You can safely apply oil of vitamin-E over nasty scares which scare all the young ones. If garlic and parsley are given orally, it will have very salutary effect. As a last atternative, herbal teas also have great healing and sober effect if served internally. Mild teas prepared from marigold, lemon balm, catnip, basil, camomile, penny royal or Vervain can be used with advantage several times during the day—adding some honey and/or cinnamon. Serve only the said teas, fresh fruits, salads lean meat or fish. Leave out pulses, spices, condiments, fatty foods, carbohydrates and even salt.

In olden times black currents, molasses, figs were, and even now, used frequently but must be taken in moderate and infrequent doses. If the kid is too young, the said food items may be boiled and served, when cool. Black berry raspberry and Rhubarb (this being the most effcacious of all) will quench excesssive thirst. Orange and carrot juices can also be given.

Measles

This is also common disease engulfing almost all the children. To begin with the patient has some cough and feverishness, besides remaining listless, running nose, occasional headache, weepy eyes, some complaint relating to stomach, pains, aches and other symptoms. After 3-4 days the patient has a drop in temperature but small white ulcers appear in the mouth which is followed by slight feverishness again. Then a red rash appears behind the ear and across the forehead, but onset in rather gradual, after which rashes begin to look like a boiled lobster. After 3-4 days the rashes start disapperaing alongwith fall in temperature but ear-ache, cough and eye soreness do persist. If the mentioned last three symptoms appear or persist, you must inform your attending physician without any delay. Protect other children from the attack and keep them away from the patient. Only saving grace about measles is that it doesn't attack a person again in one's lifetime. Diet is the same as mentioned under 'Chicken Pox'. To hasten quicker recovery, give extra doses of vitamin-C, preferably orange or Mousambi Juice. Grape is, by far, the best fruit that eliminates, toxins, builds up resistance powder, provides minerals and vitamins.

The parents are warned to contact their physicians in case of any disorder like pneumonia, imparied vision or tendency to continuous ear infections. Lavender and honey mixture should be used as a throat gargle.Chest troubles can be warded off by wine of Ipecacuanha. In my opinion, Vasaka and liquorice syrup will meet of the cough and chest disorders and complications.

To make a calming tea use yarrow, red clover flowers and vervain. Following ingredients may be utilised to prepare a soothing and curative tea. For dried herbs take 15 gms and for fresh herbs take 25 gm of each of the undernoted herbs—

Balm Melessa

Marigold

Elderflowers

Peppermint

Simmer (For 15 minutes) in one litre wter gently and take 1-2 ounces thrice a day.

Wash the eyes with a mild lotion of boric acid—3-4 times daily.

Whooping Cough (Pertussis)

This was, at one time, almost uncontrollable disorder that was agonising for the child and the parents but now the situation is well under control due to timely adherance to preventive devices. The child gets bouts of persistant coughing, leading to violent vomiting, the body turns, quite often, bluish and the child pants and gasps for fresh air. Whoop is actually a noisy convulsive drawing in of the breath following the spasmodic coughing attack, hence its nomeclation. It is an acute contagious disease affecting children (Rarely or never found in grown up adults) due to infection of the mucus lining of air passages, caused by the bacterium, hemophilis Pertussis. After an incubation period of 1-2 weeks catarrh, mild fever, coughing and loss of appetite set in and persist for another 1-2 weeks. The cough becomes paroxysmal when series of short attacks are followed by (involuntary) drawing in of the breath that produces the whooping sound. Bleeding from mouth and/or nose often follows a paroxysm which state lasts for another two weeks or so but the child remains infectious throughout and the infection can spread to healthy children also, if not properly guarded. After 2-3 weeks, symptoms decline, but the cough persists for many weeks. The affected child is highly suceptible to tuberculosis and pneumonia but the symptoms are alleviated, intensity and severity reduced by timely immunization (know as DPT vaccume).

If the whopping is triggered by starts in the bud of the year, it will last till the leaves fall, and the child will have repeated attacks every year at the same time. Rituals and religious convictions and beliefs apart, no nostrum should be practised.

A mild tea processed from Chamomile is, by far, the best sedative. It will keep the child quiet, calm and sedate, as it is anti-sposmadic also (1 TSP dose). Similarly lemon and catnip (1 TSP or even TBSP) tea (mild) can also be tried. Add some honey also.

As for another soothing solutions, infuse 20 gm of thyme in 500 ml of boiling water, strain and mix honey (1 TSP for smaller children and 1 TBSP for older children), and give 3-4 times a day. Avoid milk if the child develops any revulsion thereto. Tea of marjoram, hawkweed will help to bring down fever—dose being as indicated above or simmer one cleaned head of lettuce in 600 ml water for 20-25 minutes and serve thrice daily. To cleanse nose, throat and mouth, give grape juice—it will also loosen tenacious and trapped cough and also enhance general resistance. Slippery Elm's powdered bark (mixed with honey & water) is an excellent food and tonic. Apply some drops of eucalyptus, after mixing it to essential oil of cypress or pine and almond oil.

Mumps

This a virus infection that affects mostly the children between the age of 5-15 years, so to say, but adults are, by no means, immune. After the exposure, headache, fever and vomiting may surface and precede a typical swelling of the parotid salivary glands. Gland, generally swells on one side of the face but the other may also swell. The swelling subsides generally after 2-3 days but the infection may spread to other salivary glands, brain, testicles, pancreas. In some male adults mumps may even cause steritity.

Locally apply hot compresses or flannel strips, dipped in tincture of Calendula or Arnica or saturate a cloth in warm St. John's Wort oil. Essential oil of sage/lavender, mixed with sunflower oil, may be rubbed over throat and neck. Make sure that only plenty of liquids, in the form of vegetables or/and fruit juices (excepting, of course, juice of lemon and orange) grape juice should be substituted for lemon and orange juices. Further, ensure smooth movement of bowels, that is there ought to be no constipation.

Use Nettle or Dandelion tea by using 25 gm of either of the herbs to 600 ml of boiling water. Alternatively, infuse 25 gms each of marsh mellow and chammoile (flowers) tea and allow it to cool. When cooled, add a pinch of cinnamon or ginger or nutmeg powder and 2 TSPs or more of honey.

Caution : Body system of infants and children is quite sensitive, hence mothers of children, who are breast-fed, should be give light and moderate doses. If, for any reason, the child is not able to ingest any liquid, let the breast-feeding mother take adult dose of the prescribed/suggested recipes. In any case, the child must not be served anything against his will or when he shows any revulsion. In your eagerness to see your child cured earlier, never overdose him or increase frequency of dosage. If any disorder takes place in extreme of heat or cold, the child must be fully protected from onslaught and dangers of weather conditions. If you are using teas or infusions or hot liquids, make sure that child's mouth and throat do not get burnt—hence serve only lukewarm liquids in wintry conditions and slightly cold in hot weather conditions. What is moderately hot or cold for you, may prove extremely hot and cold for the child, as body temperatures are quite at variance in adults and children. Ideal hot or cold drink should be akin to mother's breast milk. In case, never use ice to cool the drinks or fridge the same.

(14)

NERVOUS DISORDERS

A ny event, that does not fall and adjust within the ambit of our sustaining power and resistance, is bound to recoil on most of us in the form of any one of symptoms like.

Anxiety

Depression

Low and Doomed Spirits

Schizophrenia

Stress

Anxiety and allied disorders : Truly speaking these are nomenclated states of various mood upsets that tend to or actually overpower us. Medicines are not going to take hold of those patients who have lost their willpower or whose energy to fight with the oddities of life have waned or actually disappeared. Unless a positive attitude to life and its variable events are inculcated, no reform or betterment can ensue. Hence, try to meet the odd and unfavourable situations in life with grit and determination, strong willpower and dexterity and never (or at least try to) wilt under pressure of mental strain.

Remember, mind is the driving and motivating force of our actions, reflexes and reactions. If you have a strong mind, any mental upset is not likely to adversely affect your. But, if your mind is ailing, your body cannot remain healthy. Cause of anxiety and stress related problems are merely symptomatic appearances whose underlying cause lies on elsewhere and, when the cause has been isolated or discerned, cure is not difficult. Physical stress is merely a fal-out symptom of mental stress and, at times, the symptoms get intermingled to create a confused state. Insomnia, nightmares, depression, phobia, restivity, sweating, palpitation, aches and pains in various parts of the body, panicky states, hastiness, skin eruptions etc. are an off-shoots of our disturbed mental faculties. The wiser men compromise with the situations, whereas the weaker ones simply wilt under pressure. I am delibarately dealing with mental symptoms because most of our physical disorders emanate from mental distrubance. Howsoever, you may try to conceal your feeligns and expressions, your eyes and facial expressions will reveal the struggle taking place within your mind.

Try to relax and soothe your agitated nerves and wayward thoughts. Try to engage yourself in some sport, hobby, cultural/social programme, family affair, friend circle, outing with your family members, in reading books and magazines, viewing, T.V. enjoying music, some indoor/outdoor activity, fruitful chat or gossip. Adopt following measures.

- Fennel, marjoram, holy basil, thyme, hyssop, sage and rosemary will relieve your tension and anxiety.

- When hormonal balance seems to have been disturbed, massage with essential oil of sage and also drink sage tea.

- You can also use Chamomile, bergot, vervain, orange and lavender in the form of essential oils or cooking, or else such oils can also be used in bath and massage. The herbal ingredients are also sedative and digestive.

- Cederwood, frankincense, geranium, neroli, and

coriander are all spicy healing oils which are calming, when used in the bath.

You can pick the one that suits you the best. (Massage and oil bath techniques have been detailed in earlier chapters which see)

- Whenever you feel tired take a TSP of honey in hot water.

- To get rid of persistent insomnia and restlessness, mix a TSP of honey to a glass of warm milk with a dash of Cinnamon.

- Whenever you feel you are beginning to feel depressed, tense or agitated boil 3 heads or cones of Hops and take it hot. It will also remove anxiety and insomnia. *Tea to soothe and heal troubled spirits.*

- Try following recipe to calm anxiety, turmoil or upset, to divest the head of fuziness and disordered stomach.

Lime Flowers
Camomile Flowers
Marigold Flowers
Blossoms of Hibiscus
Peppermint Leaves
and Vervain
⎦ Each 25 gms, but use only dried ingredients

Lapsang souchang Tea
Fenugreek seeds (Whole)
⎦ 1 TSP each

Pound all the ingredients and mix, store in an airtight container of dark colour. Put in one TSP of the powder in about 300 ml of water and allow to stand for 5% minutes or so, after which it should be strained. You may also add, after straining, a slice of lemon and a TSP of honey to make it more palatable and beneficial.

- To soothe the agitated and turmoiled nerves grate 1 TSP (each) of dried mint and valerian root, ½ TSP each of dried lavender flower and chamomile and all

187

the ingredients of boiling water and strain for fifteen minutes. Normal and usual dose is 200 ml (or a glass), to be taken thrice daily, and continued for seven days only.

- To relieve debility, anxiety and stress, prepare tea from 1 TSP each of and black current, 1 TSP each of borage leaves and dandelion and nettle tops—add to 500-600 ml boiling water, steep the green ingredients in water for 5 minutes, strain and add honey and lemon to the drink in doses of 150-200 ml daily for 7 days only.

- For a healthy and nourishing 'breakfast, especially for the young students, whose examinations are fast approaching, take one TSP of oats and mix with 45 ml (3 TBSP) of cold water and leave to stand for whole of night. The yield should be blended with 3 TBSP of plain live yogurt, 1 TSBP of lemon juice, 1 TSP of honey, some finely chopped nuts, (fully washed and cleansed). If the kids do not relish the said preparation, they can be served with oat porridge.

- Another ideal breakfast food, as follows, is an excellent all-round nutritious, healthy and memory tonic.

Fat Juicy Raisins	-	450 gms
Porridge of Oats	-	450 gms
Wheat Flakes	-	225 gms
Mixed Nuts (chopped)	-	100 gms
(excepting of course, peanuts)		
Wheat Germ	-	100 gms
Dried Banana Chips (Crushed)	-	100 gms
Sunflower Seeds	-	50 gms
Pumpkin Seeds	-	50 gms
Sesame Seeds	-	100 gms

All the forementioned articles should be mixed together, for being served with chopped fresh season fruit, stewed dried food, milk or yoghurt. The quantity will suffice to meet breakfast requirement of a small family (say 4-5 members) for a week. The quantity, in each ingredient, can be reduced or increased, in view of size of a family and the days for which it is required/ intended to be utilised. You can try anyone of the suggested devices suiting your pocket and convenience.

Depression

Anxiety breeds depression or it is simply an offshoot of anxiety states of various etiologies that stem from lack of vitamin B-6 or Vitamin-B complex itself, from sudden shock, unwelcome and unexpected bad news or intake of certain medicines, particularly antibiotics or mood elevator soft (escape) routes. Some latent or patent phobia can also trigger depression. Any event which upsets your rhythm of normal life stream will suffice to depress your spirits, and make you gloomy. To take umbrage under the garb of sedatives and tranqulliseres or so-called mood stabilizers, consumption of liquorous drinks, addicting yourself to drugs or sleeping in excess of your requirement are, in fact, no solutions—they are simply escapist routes or damaging short-cuts which can neither treat nor cure the basic cause of malady. You won't wilt under depression if you have the capacity to withstand onslaught of unexpected episodes of life. If you are a 'get-goer' and, above that, a good fighter you are not likely to succumb to pressure of such disturbing events. As for my experience goes, 'stickers' are more prone to depression due to their uncompromising, unreleting and obstinate temperament and snobbish behaviour. If you learn the art of coping with depressed states with a cheerful, receptive and 'Doesn't matter' approach, you won't have to resort to artificial means to seek a fabricated and unreal reprieve. Try 'Shavasana' (corpse pose) to get rid of depression. You can take to morning walk, hot bath, massage with essential oils, meditation, light but nutritive meals. Try anyone of the undermentioned

189

changes, such as alternatives Nature's greenery, plantation, rather entire vegetation on earth, water-falls, sea shores, river banks, hills and mountains, change of place and environment will serve as a soothing balm to your agitated tempers. The youngest child in the family is, by far, the best source of tension/depression reliever. If you can learn to feel like a child, play like a child and behave you will gain a lot, without spending even a penny. Laughter is another tonic for warding off or getting rid of depression. 'Happy go lucky' persons rarely wilt under depression and, if at all they do, extent of severity and intensity is neither disturbing nor damaging—as they know well how to laugh away their problems. So, be happy, learn the art of happiness from an innocent child, mix up with people, exchange your views, have a confidant to whom you can open out your mental reservations, laugh away problems, avoid display of nervosity, as you cannot change the world around you but can certainly change your attitude and approach to your life, by keeping yourself happy and also sharing your happiness with others around you. You cannot afford to be a Robinson Crusoe or a social recluse. If you expect others to listen to your woeful problems you should, likewise, spare time to listen to others also.

You can take anyone or more of the following devices, in relation to food & herbs :-

- Take 1-2 fresh oranges in your breakfast or at the time of lunch (before or after). If you take it an hour before lunch, it will increase your appetite, but if taken after meals, it will digest your food quickly, apart from soothing you.

- Take herbal teas from vervain, valerin, lemon balm, chamomile (any one) by taking infusions.

- Remember, walnut is shaped like our brain, as a leave of margosa is shaped like our pancreas, heart like an apple. So, consume walnuts in moderate quantity (but avoid it in extreme heat) so as to nourish and strengthen your fatigued brain.

- Marigolds cheer the doomed spirits and are pleasing to the eyes; hence grow this bright flower in pots on windowstill.

- Take a TBSP of Apple Cider vineger with honey, diluted in a cup of warm water as first thing in the morning and last thing at night. It is an all-round best tonic for the brain and body.

- If you can place a lavender pillow underneath your head, you will enjoy a sound, refreshing and peaceful sleep.

- Use plenty of Sage and Rosemary herbs—either in the form of tea or in cooking.

All the above-mentioned foods and herbs are useful only when you have constructive and healthy approach to life—they only aid in treating the disorder but cannot substitute self-reform and self-management. No doubt, they will pave the way and facilitate the process of self-descipline.

Insomnia (Sleeplessness or Lack of Sleep)

Duration of sleep has no relation to sound sleep, as you may feel tired, agitated, depressed even after a long sleep but some feel fresh and happy even after a short nap. Following factors account for lack or absence of sleep viz,

— Anxiety, Nervous tension, Depression.

— Some, acute or chronic illness

— Discontinuance (Sudden) of sleeping pills, drugs, drinks or even certain foods.

— Total darkness, dazzling lights or insufficient light.

— Poor ventillation and lack of fresh air (for want of proper cross-ventillation).

— Too hot or too cold room temperature.

— Too soft or too hard bed.

191

— Indigestion, flatulence, asthmatic bouts, headache, hypertension, pain and aches in the whole body or any particular part.

— Fasting or indiscreet indulgence in heavy and excessive food than is actually required.

— Sleeping late at night or missing your normal sleep time (while reading, viewing T. V. listening to music etc.)

— Travelling at a stretch and without taking any rest, or else leading a sedentary and inactive life.

— Lack of physical activity or taking to excessive physical exercises than the body can acutally endure.

— Unbalanced diet that is deficient in vitamins, minerals, and dairy/poultry products, fruits and green vegetables.

— Total abstinence and too much indulgence in sex or simply dwelling on sexual fantasies.

— Use of too much of spices, peppers, chillies, fats, condiments, acidic fruits etc.

Whatever be the cause of insomnia, never take any sleeping pill, neither overeat nor keep on fast at a stretch, avoid using, drugs and alcohol, avoid taking heavy, fat enriched and fried foods, late-night keeping. Some people habitually take milk, tea or coffee at bed time daily and if, for any reason, they are unable to take any of such beverages, sleep will remain a distant dream for them.

Debility/General Weakness

It is not a disease but simply a symptom which can be caused by :

• Low haemogbolin in the blood.

• Some wasting and chronic disease like tuberculosis, asthma, cancer, diabetes etc.

192

- Repeated pregnancies and profuse and frequent menstruation.

- Poor diet and low nutrional quality.

- Some accident-resulting in excessive bleeding.

- Loss of appetite (Anorexia)

- Heavy and exhausting workload, without any food supplementation.

- Worry, anxiety, family-related and social problems.

First of all replenish your diet with green and leafy vegetables like beets, spinach, cabbage, green mint, coriander, tomato, potato etc., add fruits like grapes, mangoes, pomegrante, bael, coconut (preferably coconut water) orange, dates, currents, dry fruits and seeds, poultry and milk products and fats. If your diet is fully balanced, there is no need to take extra doses of Iron, Vitamins, Folic acid, Minerals, Carbohydrates.

Ginseng an old herb which can invigorate entire body, raise Hb level in blood and improve general resistance, by building up defence machenism. Dock is another dependable herbal tonic that is rich in iron content. Prepare Dock-wine as detailed hereunder.

Dock Root	-	175 gm
Jumper Berries	-	7 gm
Raw Cane Sugar	-	100 gm
Liquorice Wood	-	15 gm and
Robust Red Wine	-	2 litres (non-chemical quality)

Mix all the ingredients, listed above, and put in a container of china-clay, cover the same and place in a very slow oven. Continue to heat the mixture gently, till the contents are reduced to half the quantity. To gain complete health, drink one sherry glass (for two weeks) in the morning only. You can also steep six springs of rosemary in one bottle of sweet (white) wine and keep the same sealed for two weeks whereafter take one wine glass, as a tonic, daily (once only).

If perparation of the said liquids is a problem, take daily a mixed juice of orange, promegrate or mint, beet, carrot & lemon, adding black salt to enhance taste. Juice of cabbage, turnip, tomato and spinach will also remove non-specific anaemia/debility.

Preventive and Curative remedies to get rid of Nightmares

Nightmares are the result of some frightening dreams, stemming from dreadful experiences of recent past or immediate present. When too much horror novels are watched, novels read, and stories of frightening nature are heard or when one sees some horrible figures during dreams. Some sort of fear psychosis, whether real or imaginary, lies at the back of such nightmares. Certain psychic setbacks aslo trigger horrifying dreams. Some people believe that if plenty of water is drunk, immediately before going to bed, at night, it may result in nightmares. Following recipes may banish chances of nightmares, but these should be tried not regularly but only in an emergency, to get rid of nightmares.

Infuse ¼ TSP each of vervain, lemon balm, peppermint and 1 TSP of grated valerian root for about fifteen minutes, in a cup of boiling water, and sweeten the some with honey. Other useful teas are : sage, lady's mentle, fennel, dill, horse's tail or chamomile with addition of a pinch of cinnamon.

Anything, which is difficult to digest or is not suitable to some person, or excessive intake of cheese peanuts can also lead to nightmares. Mix ground seeds of one cardamom pod; add two drops of peppermint oil, a pinch of soda-bicarbonate and 1 TSP of sugar in a cup of boiling water. It will rectify the ill-efeccts of wrong eating. In all situations, avoid the precipitating factors (known factors).

It is reminded once again that the patient has to pick up the best suited recipe, keeping in mind his allergic reactions, suitability or otherwise of a particular recipe or any ingredient, unfavourable and inimical to health, forming part of the parent recipe. It is simply a pick-and-choose approach and you have to decide yourself in this regard. In case of any doubt or/and confusion, consult a herbalist

ALLERGIES AND ALLERGIC REACTIONS

Any factor like food, climatic changes, irritants, emotional and metnal upsets, chemical air-related pollutants, water impurities, noise pollutions, are some of the factors than can cause reactions in certain individuals, but not all the individuals. Lack of resistance to certain ingredients surfaces in the form of allergies of various eliotogies we cannot do much about certain allergic factors but food allergies can be contained by suitable avoidance. For the sake of convenience allergies can be divided into following groups/classes, viz:

Food Allergies

These comprise of allergies emanating from and caused by unpleasant reactions such as Dairy products, eggs, tomatoes, strawberries, yeast, white flour, fish, shellfish, pork, colourings and preservatives, artificial sweeteners, flavour enhancers, mint, beets, spinach, jak fruit etc. Certain foods are known causes of allergies but a few of them cause allergic reactions when they are combined other foods, but not when used singally.

Drug Allergies

It is now a common knowledge that anti-biotics, any one of the vitamins out of the B-complex group, iron tonics or injections, even unhygienic and infected injection syringes and needles, certain skin ointments, creams, lotions beauty-care ingredients like facial creams, talcum powders, scents, deodocrants, lip sticks, nail polishes, hair dyes etc. are potent precipitatory allergic causatives. Once you have discerned the allergy causing item, you can avoid the same and, thus, stay free from such reactions.

Contact Allergies/External Allergies

Under this heading the allergies caused by certain plants, flowers, pollens, fragrant oils, soaps, hair oils, facial creams/lotions, talcum powders, chemicals, contact (direct) with certain chemicals, scents, essential oils, perfumes, mosquito repellants, cosmetics, perfumes, disinfectants and deodorants, washing and bathing soaps, washing powders, can be placed. The list is too exhaustive to mention. Some of the causatives mentioned, under. Drug allergies, have been deliberately repeated since they fall under this category too.

Allergies of other kinds

Dust, smoke, extreme heat or cold, or even dry weather, contaminated water, polluted air due to emittance of poisonous gases by thermal power houses, chemicals released into air by chemical units, toxins released into rivers, ponds, rivulets, canals, oceans, water reservoirs. Human excretions, like faeces and urine, also contribute a lot in vitiating water purity and air. Water contamination is the main source for causing digestive upsets, diarrhoea, cholera, anorexia, flatulence, flatulent colic, acidity etc.

Nervous and Emotional Problems

It is not an easy task to change the mode of one's style, way of thinking, family circumstances, family and finance related problems. Stress, depression, anxiety, nervosity, nervous breakdown, easily wilting under emotional or circumstantial stress, are some of the symptoms of emotional upsets which are potent precipiptating factors in enhancing ill-effects of other allergic factors.

Disorders Caused by Various Allergies

— Allergic cough (Probably of nervous origin)
— Sneezing, running form nose, cold, soreness of eyes, nose, throat and mouth, irritation and inflammation of these organs.

— Asthma, wheezing, trapped phlegm, bronchitis, tonsillitis etc.

— Diarrhoea/watery loose motions, cholera, digestive upsets.

— Nausea and vomiting, water brash.

— Skin disorders like eczema, skin rashes, urticaria/ hives, pruritis, itching, pimples.

— Choking, gagging, dyspnoea, irritating and persistant cough, or even bouts of cough.

— Pains and aches in various parts of the body due to extreme fatigue, caused by lack of resistance triggered by outside factors.

Avoidance and Pre-emptive Measures

• Avoid foods, prepared commercially in hotels, food jaunts, restaurants, road side eating places. Avoid fast foods, chats, exposed foods, drinks, cheap cold beverages, stale foods and fruits.

• Protect your body from sudden thermic changes like extreme cold, heat, rains. Wear clothes in accordance with the weather conditions.

• Boil water first, then let it cool. Always consume boiled water and avoid taking water from open ponds, chemically polluted water resources. If you consume pure food and water, you will be freed from most of the allergic reactions and other fallout symptoms.

• Burn herbs and spices to purify and disinfect your house, instead, of harping on the use of artificial air purifiers/sprays.

• Do not embroil children in your stressful and anxious mental states, rather keep them free from such mental upsets.

- Ensure high standard of personal hygiene.

- Use honey, holy basil, cumin, coriander, cinnamon, mint, fresh oranges, grapes and coconut to build up resistance to outside reactions.

- Lemon, Amla are the best sources of vitamin-C. If you consume these in moderate quantity, as essential food items, your daily diet, you are not likely to be overtaken by allergies.

- Swimming, sea-side walking, or else morning walk, inhalation of pure and fresh air, daily bath, daily exercise will fortify your body to wage a war against all allergic reactions and help you to lead a hassle free life

- Eat plenty of seasonal fruits, green and leafy vegetables or juices of fruits and vegetables, whey, curd, milk, fish oil or fish (if you are not allergic).

- Avoid fattening substances as they help to add extra weight to your body, thus lowering your resistance to fight infections.

- Drink plenty of pure and fresh water, or still better boiled water. An elderly person had suggested use of hot water with meals to ward off diseases. Try to maintain electrolytic balance in the body, especially when there is water-sodium depletion, caused by excessive sweating and loose watery motions. It is more important for infants, pregnant ladies and aged persons.

- Avoid spieces condiments and extra fats during cooking. As a rule boiled vegetables retain essential vitamins and minerals but cooking destroys all of them.

- Modertate use of fats is not forbidden but excessive

use, in heavy quantities, must be avoided. Use unsaturated vegetables oils according to suitability.

- Use whole wheat, unpolished rice, as finely ground wheat and polished rice can and often do impede peristaltic action of bowels by causing constipation.

Herbal Recipes

- Teas of chamomile, lime, mallow will not only improve immunity level but will also purge out toxic matters from the body.

- Sage and chamomile teas inculcate feeling of well-being, provide calmness and soothness.

- Take 2-4 garlic pearls daily to antidote ill-effects of infective disorders.

- Use coriander, mint, onion, garlic, lemon juice, ginger, black salt, green chillies to prepare a digestive and palatable paste which can be used alongwith other food items. Even use of one lemon, at each meal time, will build up resistance and provide immunity from most of the infections.

It is claimed that if your food is poisoned, the colour of foods items (cooked) will get changed when lime juice is added to them.

- Take a glass of lukewarm water and mix a TSP each of honey and lime juice which should be taken daily in the morning, on empty stomach.

- Those of you who can afford and tolertae, should warm a TSP or desi ghee and mix five peeled and crushed almonds, raw sugar (1 TSP), black pepper, (5 nos), water melon and musk melon seeds (2 gms each). It is an excellent tonic to raise body's resistance to various infections, serve as a tonic and also remove constipation, dispel cough, cold, sore throat and chest infections. You can cut down or raise the quantities according to individual requirements. The recipe is meant to be taken in the morning, on empty stomach, daily. In winter only, you can add 4-6 flakes of saffron also. Do not be carried away be sceptics.

- If tolerated well, a glassful of hot milk, taken at the time of retiring to bed, will induce sound sleep, remove constipation, improve digestion and also impart strength to the body and tranquility to mind, remove fatigue and aches/pains from the body. To hasten quick effect, you can add a TSP of desi ghee and almond paste (say of 5 big almonds). If diarrhoea ensues, do not use ghee but almonds may not be discontinued.]

Self-Management of Allergies

Certain food items, fruits, drinks, spices, condiments, atmosphere changes, water pollutions can be controlled without much extra-effort, though air pollution is difficult to control. Prevention & precaution are the best forms of defence. You cannot force the vehicle owners to take measures to stop emittance of poisonous smoke/fumes from their vehicles, but can protect your respiratory tract by wearing a cloth mask and binoculars for eyes and skin protection.

Similary, you can use your window to grow flowers and creepers so as to let in oxygen and let out poisonous elements/gases. To free your house from germs, you can burn the herbs and spices for the purpose. Always wash the vegetables and fruits before consuming them. Similarly, as you fully know, infection so enters from mouth also, you can wash your hands before you consume anything—this is not merely a ritual, it is of paramount importance for keeping your body disease free and healthy.

It is a misplaced notion to preach that able-bodied persons need not undertake any exercise, either indoor or outdoor. If health is in order, exercise must be undertaken regularly—as regularly as you take your meals. Your life pattern must be guided by following imperatives viz

1. Regularity in food habits, timing for proper rest.
2. Performing daily chores, including your official work, punctually.
3. Physical acitivity in any form, but it must be regular and sustainable, within the ambit of your physical capacity/endurance
4. Fixed hours of sleep, rest, relaxation, prayers, meditation and self-introspection.

If you are able to strike a perfect balance between food, work and rest/relaxation, you are not likely to encounter any major health problem.

(15) Hindi Equivalents For Herbs

Names of most of the herbs are not fully known to many persons, because each herbs is called and known by different names in different regions and languages. It is not possible to give equivalent names of each herb in each language. But, Hindi names are generally popular among the masses, hence only Hindi equivalents to English names are being mentioned below. In the earlier chapter most herbs have been given their Latin, Roman or common English names.

Name of the herb	Hindi Equivalent
Alfalfa	अल्फ़ालफ़ा
Aniseed	Vilayati Saunf, विलायती सौफ़
Arjun	Kahu, काहू

Ash Gourd	Petha, पेठा
Ashoka	Ashoka, अशोक
Asafoetida	Heing, हींग
Babul	Keekar, कीकर
Bamboo	Bans, बाँस
Banyan	Barh, बड़
Bael fruit	Bel, बेल / बिल
Balleric Myrobalam	Bahera, बहेड़ा
Bay Berry	Kaiphal, कायफल
Bitter Chamomile	Babunah, बबूना
Black Nightshade	Makoy, मकोय
Betel Leaves	Paan, पान (पत्ता)
Betel Nut	Supaari, सुपारी
Bishop's weed	Ajwain, अजवायन
Butea	Palash, पलाश
Calamus	Vach, वच
Colchicum	Hirantootiya, हिरनतूतिया
Chalmogra	Garuda Phal, गरूड़ फल
Caraway seeds	Kala zeera, काला जीरा
Cassia	Amaltas, अमलतास
Cardamom	Chhoti Ilayachi, छोटी इलायची
Celery	Ajwain Ka Patta, अजवायन का पत्ता
Castor Seeds	Arandi Ke Beej, अरण्डी के बीज
Chebutic Myroblam	Harad, हरड़, हर्रा
Cinnamon	Dalchini, दालचीनी
Clove	Lavang/Laung, लवरंग, लौंग

Chicory	Kasni, कासंनी / काशनी
Coriander	Dhaniya, धनिया
Cumin seeds	Jeera, जीरा
Dandelion	Kukaraundha, ककरौंधा
Datura	Dhatura, धतूरा
Devil's Tree	Shaitan-Ka-Jhar, शैतान का झाड़
Digitalis	Tilpushapi, तिलपुष्पी
Dill	Soya, सोया
Euphorbia	Lal Dudhi, लाला दूधी
Ephendra	Asmania, असमानिया
Fenugreek	Methi, मेथी
Fennel	Saunf, सौंफ़
Garlic	Lahsun, लहसून
Ginger	Adrak, अदरक
Hyssop	Zoofa Yabis, जूफा यबीस
Henna	Mehandi, मेहन्दी
Hog Weed	Punarnava, पुनर्नवा
Holi Basil	Tulsi, तुलसी
Indian Gooseberry	Amla, अमला
Indian Hemp	Bhaang, भांग
Indian Sorrel	Amboti-ki-Patti, अंबोटी की पत्ती
Indian Spikenard	Jatamanshi, जटामांसी
Indian Berbery	Rasaunt, रसौंत
Indian Aloe	Ghee Kanwar, घी कुँआ / धृत कुमारी
Isabghula	Isabgole, ईसबगोल
Indian Podophyllum	Papari, पपड़ी

Indian Sarasaparrila	Anantmool, अनंतमूल
Kantakari	Kateli, कटेली
Leadwort	Chitra, चित्रा
Lemon Balm	Bililotan, बिलिलोटन
Linseed	Alsi, अलसी
Liquorice	Mullethi, मुलेठी
Margosa	Neem, नीम
Marigold	Zergul, जेरगुल
Marjoram	Maridu Daru, मृदुदारू
Madhuca	Mahua, महुआ
Nutmeg	Jaiphal, जायफल
Parsley	Ajomod Ajwain, अजमोद / अजवायन
Parslane	Kulfa, कुल्फा
Picrorhiza	Kutki, कुटकी
Pepal/Peepal	Peepal, पीपल
Pepper	Kali Mirch, काली मिर्च
Poppy Seeds	Khas-Khas, खसखस
Rauwolfia	Sarpagandha, सर्पगंधा
Rhubarb	Revant Chini, रेवंत चीनी
Rough Chaff	Chirchita, चिरचिटा
Saffron	Kesar, केसर
Snake Gourd	Chachinga, चचिंगा
Safe	Shafakush, Tulsibandh शफ़ाकश, तुलसीबंध
Sandalwood	Sandal, संदल
Saussurea	Kooth, कूठ
Tamarind	Imli, इमली

Trailing Eclipta	Bhangra, भांगरा
Turmeric	Haldi, हल्दी
Turpeth	Nisoth, निशोथ

MISCELLANEOUS HERBS WITH HINDI EQUIVALENTS

Asparagus	Safed Moosli, सफ़ेद मूसली
Barley	Jau, जौ
Bay	Kaiphal-ka-Pauda, कायफल का पौधा
Bayberry	Kaiphal, कायफल
Bergomat	Zabir, ज़बीर
Betony	Chhittran Parni, छिन्राण पर्णी
Birch	Bait/Bhojapatra, बैत/भोजपत्रा
Black Berry/Rose Apple	Jamun, जामुन
Black Current	Kali Rasbhary, काली रसभरी
Black Thorn	Krishan Kantak, कृष्ण कंटक
Bladderwrack	Shaival, शैवाल
Borage	Pathar churi, पत्थर चूड़ी
Burdock	Beej Kosh, बीज कोष
Camomile	Babuna-ka-Pandha, बबूना का पौधा
Centuary	Bans Keora, बांस केवड़ा
Chickweed	Safed Phulki, सफ़ेद फुलकी
Cleavers	Lipatni Ghas, लिपटनी घास
Clover	Teen Pattiya Ghas, तीन पत्तिया घास
Coltsfoot	Desi Surajmukhi, देसी सूरजमुखी
Cranberry	Karaunda, करौन्दा

Crane's Bill	Jungli Geranium, जंगली जिरेनियम
Eyebright (herb)	Doodhi, दूधी
Figs	Anjeer, अंजीर
Flax/Linseed	Alsi, अलसी
Ground Ivy	Bhui, भुई
Hibiscus	Jayakusum, जयकुसुम
Honey suckle	Madhumalati Lata, मधुमालती लता
Horehound	Pahari Gainda, पहाड़ी गैंदा
Kale	Bandgobbi/Karamkalla, बंदगोभी / करमकल्ला
Linchen/Iceland Moss	Himadeshiya Shaivak हिमदेशीय शैवक
Marsh Mallow	Kanghi, कंघी
Nettle	Bichhoo Booti, बिच्छू बूटी
Orris	Kewara, केवड़ा
Parsnip	Chukander, चुंकन्दर
Penny Royal	Poodina Booti, पुदीना बूटी
Plantain	Kela, केला
Prunes	Sookha alucha/Aloobukhara सूखा अलूचा / आलू बुखारा
Quince	Vihi/Shriphal, वीही / श्रीफल
Red Currants	Dakh, दाख
Rue (Garden)	Brahmi Booti, ब्रह्मी बूटी
Safflower	Kusum, Kusumbha, कुसुम / कुसुम्भ
Saint John's Wort	Basant, बसंत

Sloe	Jungli Alucha, जंगली अलूचा
Turnip	Shalgum, शलगम
Valarian	Vidarikand, विदारीकन्द
Violet	Banafsha, बनफशा
Watercress	Nagadamani, नागदमनी
Yarrow	Sahastraparni, सहपर्णी
Ylang ylang	Karumugai, करूमुगई

Note : When we talk of herbs we, in fact, take into account all the parts of a plant (like leaves, flowers, bark, stem, root, rind, aerial roots, vegetables/fruits growing thereon) are used to treat various disorders of the body according their therapeutic utility. In addition to the above, certain fruits, vegetables, almost all the spices used in the kitchen, form an integral part of herbal treatment. There is hardly any ayurvedic medicine where kitchen spices are not used; hence we have to depend on whole vegetable kingdom of which herbs form merely a part.